On
Asking God
Why

Also by Elisabeth Elliot

Through Gates of Splendor
Shadow of the Almighty
Let Me Be a Woman
A Chance to Die
Discipline: The Glad Surrender
God's Guidance
The Shaping of a Christian Family
Keep a Quiet Heart
The Mark of a Man
Faith That Does Not Falter
Passion and Purity
Quest for Love
Be Still My Soul
The Journals of Jim Elliot
The Music of His Promises
No Graven Image
The Path of Loneliness
Secure in the Everlasting Arms

On
Asking God
Why

*And Other Reflections on Trusting God
in a Twisted World*

ELISABETH ELLIOT

Revell
Grand Rapids, Michigan

© 1989 by Elisabeth Elliot

Published by Fleming H. Revell
a division of Baker Publishing Group
P.O. Box 6287, Grand Rapids, MI 49516-6287

New trade paperback edition published 2006

Second printing, July 2006

Printed in the United States of America

Library of Congress Cataloging-in-Publication Data
Elliot, Elisabeth.
    On asking God why : and other reflections on trusting God in a twisted world
/ Elisabeth Elliot.
        p.   cm.
    Originally published: Old Tappan, N.J.: F.H. Revell, c1989.
    ISBN 10: 0-8007-3124-7 (pbk.)
    ISBN 978-0-8007-3124-3 (pbk.)
    1. Christian life. I. Title.
BV4501.3.E456 2006
248.4—dc22   2005023168

Do you find it difficult to approach God with the questions that are tugging at your heart?

When speaking of God, Elisabeth Elliot writes, "He is not only the Almighty. He is also our Father, and what a father does is not by any means always understood by the child."

On Asking God Why reminds us that as children of God we can bring our questions to him with all the trust of a child in his earthly parent. We are encouraged to search the Scriptures for God's answers. Among the issues Elliot contemplates are singleness, risk taking, and being judgmental of others. When we overcome our fears and decide to ask God why, he will surely give us all the answers we need.

To my husband
Lars Gren
who builds the
fences around me
and stands on all sides

Contents

Foreword

God does many things that we do not understand. Of course he does—he is God, perfect in wisdom, love, and power. We are only children, very far from perfect in anything. A true faith must rest solidly on his character and his Word, not on our particular conceptions of what he ought to do. The word *ought* presupposes an idea of justice. When God's actions do not seem to conform to our idea of justice, we are tempted at least to ask *why*, if not actually to charge him with injustice.

Thousands of years ago one of God's faithful servants, having lost practically everything, sat on an ash heap surrounded by weeping friends who were tearing up their clothes and tossing dust into the air for grief. For seven days and seven nights they were speechless in the face of Job's suffering. It was Job who broke the silence—with a long and eloquent curse. He asked the question men have asked ever since: *Why?*

Why was I not still-born?
Why did I not die when I came out of the womb?
Why was I ever laid on my mother's knees?
Why should the sufferer be born to see the light?
Why is life given to men who find it so bitter?
Why should a man be born to wander blindly, hedged in by
    God on every side?

See Job 3:11, 12, 20, 23 NEB

Written centuries later, the Psalms express similar agonized cries:

I will say to God my Rock, "Why hast thou forgotten me?" Why hast thou cast us off, O God? Is it for ever?

Psalm 74:1 NEB

There would be no sense in asking *why* if one did not believe in anything. The word itself presupposes *purpose*. Purpose presupposes a purposeful intelligence. *Somebody* has to have been responsible. It is because we believe in God that we address questions to him. We believe that he is just and that he is love, but that belief is put to severe strain as we wrestle with our pains and perplexities, with our very position in his ordered universe.

"Whence knowest thou that this thing is unjust, unless thou know what is just?" wrote St. Augustine. "Hast thou that which is just from thyself, and canst thou give justice to thyself? Therefore when thou art unjust, thou canst not be just except by turning thee to a certain abiding justice, wherefrom if thou withdrawest, thou art unjust, and if thou drawest near to it, thou art just. . . . Look back therefore, rise to the heights, go to that place where once God hath spoken, and there thou wilt find the fountain of justice where is the fountain of life. 'For with thee is the fountain of life' [Psalm 36:9]."

The pieces in this book make up a somewhat mongrel collection. Essays? Sketches? "Cautionary tales"? Those, perhaps, and some less classifiable. They touch lightly on matters of considerable weight—the mystery of suffering (losses, cancer, despair, death), the mystery of evil (abortion, divorce, euthanasia, the cult of rock "music"), and the mystery of our ordinary human condition (loneliness, hopelessness, tenderness, confusion, aging, the need for forgiveness). All but one are the expression of a single writer who owes a special debt to the author of the second chapter, "On Brazen Heavens." He is my brother, eight years my junior, to whom for the first decade or so of his life I taught everything I knew. He has been teaching me ever since. He wrote the above mentioned chapter while my husband Addison Leitch was dying. I think we share the same vision, seeking always to see things in the light of "a certain abiding justice." It is my hope that this collection will help some to "rise to the heights, go to that place where once God hath spoken," and find that Fountain of Life.

On Asking God Why

One of the things I am no longer as good at as I used to be is sleeping through the night. I'm rather glad about that, for there is something pleasant about waking in the small hours and realizing that one is, in fact, in bed and need not get up. One can luxuriate.

Between two and three o'clock yesterday morning I luxuriated. I lay listening to the night sounds in a small house on the "stern and rockbound" coast of Massachusetts. The wind whistled and roared, wrapping itself around the house and shaking it. On the quarter hour the clock in the living room softly gave out Whittington's chime. I could hear the tiny click as the electric blanket cut off and on, the cracking of the cold in the walls, the expensive rumble of the oil burner beneath me, and the reassuring rumble of a snoring husband beside me. Underneath it all was the deep, drumming rhythm of the surf, synchronized with the distant bellow of "Mother Ann's Cow," the name given the sounding buoy that guards the entrance to Gloucester Harbor.

I was thinking, as I suppose I am always thinking, in one way or another, about mystery. An English magazine which contained an interview with me had just come in the mail, and of course I read it, not to find out what I'd said to the man last spring in Swanwick, but to find out what he said I'd said. He had asked me about some of the events in my life, and I had told him that because of them I had had to "come to terms with mystery." That was an accurate quotation, I'm sure, but as I lay in bed I knew that one never comes to any final terms with mystery—not in this life, anyway. We keep asking the same unanswerable questions and wondering why the explanations are not forthcoming. We doubt God. We are anxious about everything when we have been told quite clearly to be anxious about nothing. Instead of stewing we are supposed to pray and give thanks.

Well, I thought, *I'll have a go at it*. I prayed about several things for which I could not give thanks. But I gave thanks in the middle of each of those prayers because I was still sure (the noise of the wind and ocean were reminding me) that underneath are the everlasting arms.

My prayers embraced four things:

1. Somebody I love is gravely ill.
2. Something I wanted has been denied.
3. Something I worked very hard for failed.
4. Something I prized is lost.

I can be specific about three of the things. A letter from a friend of many years describes her cancer surgery and its aftermath—an incision that had to be scraped and cleaned daily for weeks.

It was so painful that Diana, Jim, Monica, and I prayed while she cleaned it, three times and some days four times. Monica would wipe my tears. Yes, Jesus stands right there as the pain takes my breath away and my toes curl to keep from crying out loud. But I haven't asked, Why me, Lord? It is only now that I can pray for cancer patients and know how the flesh hurts and how relief, even for a moment, is blessed.

The second thing is a manuscript on which I have spent years. It is not, I believe, publishable now, and I can see no way to redeem it. It feels as though those years of work have gone down the drain. Have they? What ought I to do about this failure?

The other thing is my J. B. Phillips translation of the New Testament, given to me when I lived in the jungle in 1960 and containing nineteen years' worth of notes. I left this book on an airplane between Dallas and Atlanta several weeks ago. The stewardess brought my breakfast as I was reading it, so I laid it in my lap and spread my napkin on top of it. I suppose it slipped down beside the seat. (Stupid of me, of course, but on the same trip my husband did just as stupid a thing. He left his briefcase on the sidewalk outside the terminal. We prayed, and the prayers were almost instantly answered. Someone had picked up the briefcase and turned it in to the airline, and we had it back in a couple of hours.) I am lost without my Phillips. I feel crippled. It is as though a large segment of the history of my spiritual pilgrimage has been obliterated. It was the one New Testament in which I knew my way around. I knew where things were on the page and used it constantly in public speaking because I could refer quickly to passages I needed. What shall I do?

I have done the obvious things. Prayer is the first thing—asking God to do what I *can't* do. The second thing is to get busy and do what I *can* do. I prayed for my friend, of course, and then I sat down and wrote her a letter. I don't know what else to do for her now. My husband and I prayed together about the lost New Testament (and many of my friends prayed too). We went to the proper authorities at the airline and have been assured that everything will be done to recover it, but it has not turned up. We prayed about the bad manuscript and asked for editorial advice. It looks quite irremedial. I continue to pray repeatedly, extensively, and earnestly about all of the above. And one more thing: I seek the lessons God wants to teach me, and that means that I ask why.

There are those who insist that it is a very bad thing to question God. To them, "Why?" is a rude question. That depends, I believe, on whether it is an honest search, in faith, for his meaning, or whether it is a challenge of unbelief and rebellion. The psalmist often questioned God, and so did Job. God did not answer the questions, but he answered the man—with the mystery of himself.

He has not left us entirely in the dark. We know a great deal more about his purposes than poor old Job did, yet Job trusted him. He is not only the Almighty—Job's favorite name for him. He is also our Father, and what a father does is not by any means always understood by the child. If he loves the child, however, the child trusts him. It is the child's ultimate good that the father has in mind. Terribly elementary. Yet I have to be reminded of this when, for example, my friend suffers, when a book I think I can't possibly do without is lost, when a manuscript is worthless.

The three things are not all in the same category. The second and third things have to do with my own carelessness and failure. Yet in all three I am reminded that God is my Father still, and he does have a purpose for me, and that nothing, absolutely nothing, is useless in the fulfillment of that purpose if I'll trust him for it and submit to the lessons.

"God disciplines us for our good *that we may share his holiness.*" That is a strong clue to the explanation we are always seeking. God's purpose for us is holiness—his own holiness which we are to share—and the sole route to that end is discipline.

Discipline very often involves loss, diminishment, "fallings from us, vanishings." Why? Because God wills our perfection in holiness, that is, our *joy*. But, we argue, why should diminishments be the prerequisite for joy? The answer to that lies within the great mystery that underlies creation: the principle of life out of death, exemplified for all time in the incarnation ("that a vile Manger his low Bed should prove, who in a Throne of stars Thunders above," as Crashaw expressed it) and in the cross and resurrection ("who, for the joy that was set before him, endured a cross"). Christ's radical diminishments—his birth as a helpless baby and his death as a common criminal—accomplished our salvation.

It follows that if we are to share in his destiny, we must share in his death, which means, for us sinners, the willingness to offer up to him not only ourselves but all that goes with that gift, including the simplest, down-to-earth things. These things may be aggravating and irritating and humiliating as well as mysterious. But it is the very aggravation and irritation and humiliation that we can offer—every diminishment of every kind—so that by the grace of God we may be taught his loving lessons and be brought a little nearer to his loving purpose for us and thus be enlarged.

Somehow it's easy to understand the principle of control and denial and loss in the matter of *self*-discipline. It is perfectly plain to anyone who wants to do a difficult and worthwhile thing that he has to deny himself a thousand unimportant and probably a few hundred important things in order to do the one thing that matters most. Bishop Stephen Neill said that writing is almost entirely a matter of self-discipline. "You must make yourself write." I know. Alas. Sit yourself down, shut yourself up, restrict your enthusiasms, control your maunderings. Think. (Sir Joshua Reynolds wrote, "There is no expedient to which a man will not resort to avoid the real labor of thinking.") Diminishments. Then put things on paper—carefully. Then (and this is the part I resist more strenuously) rewrite. Cut things. Drop things you've spent hours on into the wastebasket.

I lay in bed, luxuriating in the physical bliss, cogitating on the spiritual perplexities. I could not explain why God would restore Lars' lost briefcase and not my New Testament. I could not fathom my friend's suffering or the "waste" of time. But God could. It's got something to do with that great principle of loss being the route to gain, or diminishments being the only way we can finally be enlarged, that is, conformed to the image of Christ.

"Who watched over the birth of the sea?"

The words from God's dialogue with Job came to mind as I listened to the throbbing of the ocean from my bed.

"Have you descended to the springs of the sea, or walked in the unfathomable deep?"

No, Lord, but you have. Nothing in those dark caverns is mysterious to you. Nor is anything in my life or my friend's life. I trust you with the unfathomables.

But you know I'll be back—with the usual question.

On Brazen Heavens
Thomas Howard

For about a year now I have been witness to a drama that is all too familiar to us mortal men. Someone finds he has cancer; the medical treadmill begins, with its implacable log of defeat; hope is marshaled, begins the march, is rebuffed at every juncture, flags, rouses, flags again, and is finally quietly mustered out.

And meanwhile, because the people in the drama are Christian believers, everyone is dragged into the maelstrom that marks the place where our experience eddies into the sea of the divine will. The whole question of prayer gapes open.

The promises are raked over. And over and over. "Is the primary condition enough faith on our part?" "We must scour our own hearts to see that there is no stoppage there—of sin or of unbelief." "We must stand on the promise." "We must *claim* thus and such." "We must resist the devil and his weapons of doubt."

And we leap at and pursue any and all reports and records of healings. "Look at what happened to so-and-so!" "Listen to this!" "I've just read this wonderful pamphlet." We know the Gospel accounts by heart. We agree that this work of healing did not cease with the apostolic age. We greet gladly the tales of healing that pour in from all quarters in the church—no longer only from those groups that have traditionally "specialized" in healing, but from the big, old, classic bodies in Christendom—Rome, Anglicanism, Lutheranism, Presbyterianism, and so forth. "God is doing something in our day," we hear, and we grasp at it eagerly.

And meanwhile the surgery goes on its horrific way, and the radiation burns on, week after grim week; and suffering sets in, and the doctors hedge and dodge into the labyrinthine linoleum and stainless-steel bureaucracy of the hospital world, and our hearts sicken, and we try to avert our eyes from the black flag that is fluttering wildly on the horizon, mocking us.

And the questions come stealing over us: "Where is now their God?" "Where is the promise of his coming?" "He trusted in God that he would deliver him . . ." and so on. And we know that we are not the first human beings into whose teeth the tempter and his ilk have flung those taunts.

We look for some light. We look for some help. Our prayers seem to be vanishing, like so many wisps, into the serene ether of the cosmos (or worse, into the plaster of the ceiling). We strain our ears for some word from the mount of God. A whisper will do, we tell ourselves, since clearly no bolts or thunderings have been activated by our importunity (yes, we have tried that tactic too: the "nonfaith" approach).

But only dead silence. Blank. Nothing. "But, Lord, how are we supposed to know if we're on the right track at all if we don't get some confirmation from you—some corroboration—in *any* form, Lord—inner peace maybe, or some verse springing to life for us, or some token. Please let us have some recognizable attestation to what you have said in your Book." Nothing. Silence. Blank.

Perhaps at this point we try to think back over the experience of the people of God through the millennia. There has been a whole spectrum of experience for them: glorious deliverances, great victories, kingdoms toppled, widows receiving their dead back, men wandering about in sheepskins and goatskins—

"Men wandering about in sheepskins and goatskins? What went wrong there?"

"That's in the record of faith."

"But then surely something went wrong."

"No. It is part of the log of the faithful. That is a list of what happened to the people of faith. It is about how they proved God."

The whole spectrum of experience is there. The widow of Nain got her son back and other mothers didn't. Peter got out of prison and John the Baptist didn't. Elijah whirled up to heaven with fiery horses and Joseph ended in a coffin in Egypt. Paul healed other people, but was turned down on his own request for healing for himself.

A couple of items in the Gospels seem to me to suggest something for the particular situation described in this article, where deliverance did not, in fact, come, and where apparently the juggernaut of sheer nature went on its grim way with no intervention from heaven.

One is the story of Lazarus and the other is the Emmaus account. You object immediately: "Ah, but in both those cases it turned out that the dead *were* raised." Well, perhaps there is something there for us nonetheless.

For a start, the people involved in those incidents were followers of Jesus, and they had seen him, presumably, heal dozens of people. Then these followers experienced the utter dashing of all their expectations and hopes by death. God did not, it seemed, act. He who had been declared the Living One and the Giver of Life seemed to have turned his back in this case. What went wrong? What did the household at Bethany *not* do that the widow of Nain had done? How shall we align it all? Who rates and who doesn't? Whatever it is that we might have chosen to say to them in the days following their experience of death, we would have had to come to terms somehow with the bleak fact that God had done something for others that he had not done for them.

From the vantage point of two thousand years, we later believers can, of course, see that there was something wonderful in prospect, and that it emerged within a very few days in both cases. The stories make sense. They are almost better than they would have been if the deaths had not occurred. But of course this line would have been frosty comfort for Mary and Martha, or for the two en route to Emmaus, if we had insisted to them, "Well, surely God is up to something. We'll just have to wait."

And yet what else could we have said? Their experience at that point was of the utter finality of death, which had thrown everything they had expected into limbo. For them there was no walking and leaping and praising God. No embracing and ecstatic tears of reunion. Only the silence of shrouds and sepulchers, and then the turning back, not just to the flat routines of daily life, but to the miserable duel with the tedious voices pressing in upon their exhausted imaginations with "Right! *Now* where are you? Tell us about your faith now! What'd you do wrong?"

The point is that for *x* number of days, their experience was of defeat. For us, alas, the "*x* number of days" may be greatly multiplied. And it is small comfort to us to be told that the difference, then, between us and, say, Mary and Martha's experience of Lazarus's death, or of the two on the road to Emmaus, is only a quantitative difference. "They had to wait four days. You have to wait one, or five, or seventy years. What's the real difference?" That is like telling someone on the rack that his pain is only quantitatively different from mine with my hangnail. The quantity *is* the difference. But there is, perhaps, at least this much of help for us whose experience is that of Mary and Martha and the others, and not that of the widow of Nain and Jairus and that set: the experience of the faithful *has*, in fact, included the experience of utter death. That seems to be part of the pattern, and it would be hard indeed to insist that the death was attributable to some failure of faith on somebody's part.

There is also this to be observed: that it sometimes seems that those on the higher reaches of faith are asked to experience this "absence" of God. For instance, Jesus seemed ready enough to show his authority to chance bystanders, and to the multitudes; but look at his own circle. John the Baptist wasn't let off—he had his head chopped off. James was killed in prison. And the Virgin herself had to go through the horror of seeing her Son tortured. No legions of angels intervened there. There was also Job, of course. And St. Paul—he had some sort of healing ministry himself, so that handkerchiefs were sent out from him with apparently healing efficacy for *others*, but, irony of ironies, his own prayer for *himself* was "unanswered." He had to slog through life with whatever his "thorn" was. What do these data do to our categories?

But there is more. Turning again to the disclosure of God in Scripture, we seem to see that, in his economy, there is no slippage. Nothing simply disappears. No sparrow falls without his knowing (and, one might think, caring) about it. No hair on anybody's head is without its number. Oh, you say, that's only a metaphor; it's not literal. A metaphor of *what*, then, we might ask. Is the implication there that God *doesn't* keep tabs on things?

And so we begin to think about all our prayers and vigils and fastings and abstinences, and the offices and sacraments of the church, that have gone up to the throne in behalf of the sufferer. They have vanished, as no sparrow, no hair, has ever done. Hey, what about that?

And we know that this is false. It is nonsense. All right then—we prayed, with much faith or with little; we searched ourselves; we fasted; we anointed and laid on hands; we kept vigil. And nothing happened.

25

Did it not? What angle of vision are we speaking from? Is it not true that again and again in the biblical picture of things, the story has to be allowed to *finish*?

Was it not the case with Lazarus's household at Bethany, and with the two en route to Emmaus? And is it not the case with the Whole Story, actually—that it must be allowed to finish, and that this is precisely what the faithful have been watching for since the beginning of time? In the face of suffering and endurance and loss and waiting and death, what is it that has kept the spirits of the faithful from flagging utterly down through the millennia? Is it not the hope of Redemption? Is it not the great Finish to the Story—and to all their little stories of wandering about in sheepskins and goatskins as well as to the One Big Story of the whole creation, which is itself groaning and waiting? And is not that Finish called glorious? Does it not entail what amounts to a redoing of all that has gone wrong, and a remaking of all that is ruined, and a finding of all that has been lost in the shuffle, and an unfolding of it all in a blaze of joy and splendor?

A finding of all that is lost? All sparrows, and all petitions and tears and vigils and fastings? Yes, all petitions and tears and vigils and fastings.

"But where *are* they? The thing is over and done with. He is dead. They had no effect."

Hadn't they? How do you know what is piling up in the great treasury kept by the Divine Love to be opened in that Day? How do you know that this death *and* your prayers and tears and fasts will not *together* be suddenly and breathtakingly displayed, before all the faithful, and before angels and archangels, and before kings and widows and prophets, as gems in that display? Oh no, don't speak of things being lost. Say rather that they are hidden—received and accepted and taken up into the secrets of the divine mysteries, to be transformed and multiplied, like everything else we offer to him—loaves and fishes, or mites, or bread and wine—and given back to you and to the one for whom you kept vigil, in the presence of the whole host of men and angels, in a hilarity of glory as unimaginable to you in your vigil as golden wings are to the worm in the chrysalis.

But how does it *work*? We may well ask. How *does* Redemption work?

Thomas Howard is a college professor and author of *Christ the Tiger*, *Splendor in the Ordinary*, and other books.

Singleness Is a Gift

Nearly a hundred years ago a twenty-eight-year-old woman from a windy little village on the north coast of Ireland began her missionary work in India. Amy Carmichael was single, but on the very eve of her leaving the docks, an opportunity "which looked towards 'the other life'" was presented.

Amy, with the combined reticence of being Victorian and being Irish, never said how or by whom this "opportunity" was presented. She spoke very little of matters of the heart. She was also a thoroughgoing Christian, with a soldier's determination to carry out her Commander's orders. Single life, she believed, was not only a part of those orders; it was also a gift.

She tried not to suggest in any way that her gift was superior. "Remember," she wrote, "our God did not say to me, 'I have something greater for you to do.' This life is not greater than the other, but it is different." It was simply God's call to her.

The oldest of seven children, she had been full of ideas to amuse, educate, inspire, and spiritually edify her brothers and sisters. One of these ideas was a family magazine called *Scraps*, beautifully handwritten, illustrated, and published monthly for family and friends. Before Amy was twenty, one brother knew the direction her life was taking. In a series of sketches for *Scraps* he wrote:

> Our eldest sister is the
> light of our life.
> She says that she will never
> be a wife.

Amy took as her guide the idea set forth by the apostle Paul: "The unmarried (woman) concerns herself with the Lord's affairs, and her aim is to make herself holy in body and in spirit. . . . I am not putting difficulties in your path, but setting before you an ideal, so that your service of God may be as far as possible free from worldly distractions" (1 Cor. 7:34–35 Phillips).

With all her heart she determined to please him who had chosen her to be his soldier. She was awed by the privilege. She accepted the disciplines.

"A Touch of Disappointment"

Loneliness was one of those disciplines. How—the modern young person always wants to know—did she "handle" it? Amy Carmichael would not have had the slightest idea what the questioner was talking about. "Handle" loneliness? Why, it was part of the cost of obedience, of course. Everybody is lonely in some way, the single in one way, the married in another; the missionary in certain obvious ways, the schoolteacher, the mother, the bank teller in others.

Amy had a dear co-worker whom she nicknamed Twin. At a missions conference they found that in the posted dinner lists, Twin and a friend named Mina had been seated side by side.

"Well, I was very glad that dear Mina should have Twin," Amy wrote to her family, "and I don't think I grudged her to her one little bit, and yet at the bottom of my heart there was just a touch of disappointment, for I had almost fancied I had somebody of my very own again, and there was a little ache somewhere. I could not *rejoice* in it. . . . I longed, yes *longed*, to be glad, to be filled with such a wealth of unselfish love that I should be far gladder to see those two together than I should have been to have had Twin to myself. And while I was asking for it, it came. For the very first time I felt a rush, a real joy in it, His joy, a thing one cannot pump up or imitate or force in any way. . . . Half-unconsciously, perhaps, I had been saying, 'Thou and Twin are enough for me'—one so soon clings to the gift instead of only to the Giver."

Her letter then continued with a stanza from the Frances Ridley Havergal hymn:

> Take my love, my Lord, I pour
> At Thy feet its treasure-store.
> Take myself and I will be
> Ever, only, all for Thee.

After writing this, Amy felt inclined to tear it out of the letter. It was too personal, too humiliating. But she decided the Lord wanted her to let it stand, to tell its tale of weakness and of God's strength. She was finding firsthand that missionaries are not apart from the rest of the human race, not purer, nobler, higher.

"Wings are an illusive fallacy," she wrote. "Some may possess them, but they are not very visible, and as for me, there isn't the least sign of a feather. Don't imagine that by crossing the sea and landing on a foreign shore and learning a foreign lingo you 'burst the bonds of outer sin and hatch yourself a cherubim.'"

The Single "Mother"

Amy landed in India in 1897 and spent the first few years in itinerant evangelism. She began to uncover a secret traffic in little girls who were being sold or given for temple prostitution. She prayed that God would enable her to find a way to rescue some of them, even though not one had ever been known to escape.

Several years later, God began to answer that prayer. One little girl actually escaped and came (led by an angel, Amy believed) straight to Amy. Then in various ways babies were rescued. Soon she found that little boys were being used for homosexual purposes by dramatic societies connected with Hindu temple worship. She prayed for the boys, and in a few years Amy Carmichael was *Amma* ("Mother") to a rapidly growing Indian family that, by the late 1940s, numbered about 900. In a specially literal way the words of Jesus seemed to have been fulfilled: "Everyone who has left houses or brothers or sisters or father or mother or children or fields for my sake will receive a hundred times as much and will inherit eternal life" (Matt. 19:29 NIV).

In answer to a question from one of her children who years later had become a close fellow worker, Amy described a transaction in a cave. She had gone there to spend the day with God and face her feelings of fear about the future. Things were all right at the moment, but could she endure years of being alone?

The devil painted pictures of loneliness that were vivid to her years later. She turned to the Lord in desperation. "What can I do, Lord? How can I go on to the end?"

His answer: "None of them that trust in me shall be desolate" (from Ps. 4:22 KJV). So she did not "handle" loneliness—she handed it to her Lord and trusted his Word.

"There is a secret discipline appointed for every man and woman whose life is lived for others," she wrote. "No one escapes that discipline, nor would wish to escape it; nor can any shelter another from it. And just as we have seen the bud of a flower close round the treasure within, folding its secret up, petal by petal, so we have seen the soul that is chosen to serve, fold round its secret and hold it fast and cover it from the eyes of man. The petals of the soul are silence."

Her commitment to obedience was unconditional. Finding that singleness was the condition her Master had appointed for her, she received it with both hands, willing to renounce all rights for his sake and, although she could not have imagined it at the time, for the sake of the children he would give her—a job she could not possibly have done if she had had a family of her own.

Many whose houses, for one reason or another, seem empty, and the lessons of solitude hard to learn, have found strength and comfort in the following Amy Carmichael poem:

> O Prince of Glory, who dost bring
> Thy sons to glory through Thy Cross,
> Let me not shrink from suffering,
> Reproach or loss. . . .
>
> If Thy dear Home be fuller, Lord,
> For that a little emptier
> My house on earth, what rich reward
> That guerdon* were.

*recompense; something earned or gained

4

A Look in the Mirror

Most of us are rather pleased when we catch sight of ourselves (provided the sight is sufficiently dim or distant) in the reflection of a store window. It is always amusing to watch people's expressions and postures change, perhaps ever so slightly, for the better as they look at their images. We all want the reflected image to match the image we hold in our minds (e.g., a rugged, casual slouch goes well with a Marlboro Country type; an erect, distinguished carriage befits a man of command and responsibility). We glimpse ourselves in a moment of lapse and quickly try to correct the discrepancies.

A close-up is something else altogether. Sometimes it's more than we can stand. The shock of recognition makes us recoil. "Don't tell me that's *my* voice!" (on the tape recorder); "Do I really look *that* old?" (as this photograph cruelly shows). For me it is a horrifyingly painful experience to have to stand before a three-way mirror, in strong light, in a department-store fitting room. ("These lights—these mirrors—they distort, surely!" I tell myself.) I have seen Latin American Indians whoop with laughter upon first seeing themselves on a movie screen, but I have never seen them indignant, as "civilized" people often seem to be. Perhaps it is that an Indian has not occupied himself very much with trying to be what he is not.

What is it that makes us preen, recoil, laugh? It must be the degree of incongruity between what we thought we were and what we actually saw.

People's standards, of course, differ. Usually, in things that do not matter, we set them impossibly high and thus guarantee for ourselves a life of discontent. In things that matter we set them too low and are easily pleased with ourselves. (My daughter came home from the seventh grade one day elated. "Missed the honor roll by two Cs!" she cried, waving her report card happily.) Frequently we judge by standards that are irrelevant to the thing in question. You have to know what a thing is for, first of all, before you can judge it at all. Take a can opener—how can I know whether it's any good unless I know that it was made for opening cans?

Or a church. What is it for? Recently the one I belong to held a series of neighborhood coffee meetings for the purpose of finding out what the parishioners thought about what the church was doing, was not doing, and ought to be doing. The results were mailed to us. Eighty people participated and came up with 105 "concerns and recommendations." These revealed considerable confusion as to what the church is meant to be about. "Should have hockey and basketball teams." "There is too much reference to the Bible in sermons." "The ushers should stop hunching at the doors of the church and seek out unfamiliar faces." "The rear parking lot is messy." "A reexamination of spiritual goals should be carried out." I was glad there were a few like that last one. The range of our congregational sins was pretty well covered (we didn't get into the mire of our personal ones), and as I read them over, I thought that if we just managed to straighten out these 105 things, we'd have—what? Well, something, I suppose. But not a perfect church. Not by a long shot. If by our poor standards (some of them obviously applicable to things other than churches) we picked out over a hundred flaws, how many were visible to God, "to whose all-searching sight the darkness shineth as the light"?

There are times when it is with a kind of relief that we come upon the truth. A man passing a church one day paused to see if he could catch what it was the people were mumbling in unison. He moved inside and heard the words: "We have erred and strayed from thy ways like lost sheep. We have followed too much the devices and desires of our own hearts. We have offended against thy holy laws."

Hmm, thought the man, *they sound like my kind of people*.

"We have left undone those things which we ought to have done, and we have done those things which we ought not to have done."

This is the church for me, he decided. (I don't suppose a basketball team or a blacktopped parking lot would have persuaded him.)

"Put up a complaint box and you'll get complaints," my husband says. There is something to be said for airing one's grievances, and there is a great deal to be said for not airing them, but one thing at least seems good to me—that we be overwhelmed, now and then, with our sins and failures.

We need to sit down and take stock. We need mirrors and neighborhood coffees and complaint boxes, but our first reaction may be despair. Our second, "Just who does so-and-so think he is, criticizing the church when he never even comes to church?" And we find ourselves back where we started, setting our own standards, judging irrelevantly and falsely, excusing ourselves, condemning an institution for not being what it was never meant to be, and so on.

Then there is Lent. It is a time to stop and remember. All year we have had the chance in the regular communion service to remember the death and passion of the Lord Jesus, and this once during the year we are asked, for a period of

35

six weeks, to recall ourselves, to repent, to submit to special disciplines in order that we may understand the meaning of the resurrection.

We are indeed "miserable offenders." We have done and left undone. We are foolish and weak and blind and self-willed and men of little faith. We run here, we run there, we form committees and attend meetings and attack the church and its organization and its isolation and its useless machinery and its irrelevance and ineffectiveness. But all the time it stands there, holding the cross, telling us that there is forgiveness, that we have not been left to ourselves, that no matter how shocking the image that we finally see of ourselves in the light of God's truth, God himself has done something about it all.

"He was wounded for our transgressions, he was bruised for our iniquities." For the very things we've been discussing. For the things that make us moan and groan and ask, "What's the use?"

And so Lent, simply because it is another reminder of him who calls us to forgiveness and refreshment, makes me glad.

5

Happy Birthday

You're Heading Home!

The cards on the racks simply won't fill the bill. I wander disconsolately past the "Relative," "Comic," and other categories of birthday cards, even a rack labeled, "These cards are outrageous. Prepare for shock!" What I want to wish on your birthday is not the sort of happiness that depends on the denial of the passing years, or on your undiminished power to get ever bigger and better thrills out of tall bottles or other people's beds. The cartoons are crazy. In fact, they're horrifying, in that they show what a dead-end street the desperate search for happiness usually is. The only cards that suggest the possibility of any other kind of happiness make such exaggerated claims for my feelings for you, in such soupy, mawkish language, and with such wispy or misty illustrations—no, I'm sorry, I can't bring myself to buy them.

What I want to wish you today is joy. I want you to have the happiest birthday ever. Not because you're just exactly the age you've always dreamed of being: the perfect age. Not because you'll be having the splashiest, roaringest party ever, or because you're surrounded by all your favorite fans, feeling marvelous, getting a vast pile of gorgeous gifts. I could merely wish you a happy birthday, but I'll do more than that. I'll turn my wish into prayer, and ask the Lord to give you the happiest birthday ever. I'll ask him for the kind of joy that isn't dependent on how you feel or who's there to celebrate or what's happening.

The people who write those awful cards are doing the best they can, but they haven't much to fall back on. Best to try to forget the hard facts: time *is* passing, people *are* actually growing old, happiness *is* pretty hard to come by in this old world. What is there to fall back on? Can't do a thing about the facts. The misery and loneliness and disintegration and horror are there (Edna St. Vincent Millay put it bluntly: "Death beating the door in"), but who wants to put things like that into a birthday card? Isn't it good enough to settle for cute comics, sweet sentiments, and just have fun? We can at least pretend we're happy. Forget the truth for a day. It's your birthday, and by George, we're gonna *frolic!*

That's one way to do it, but why frolic for all the wrong reasons? I love celebrations and gifts. A little dinner by candlelight in a quiet place with loved friends is my idea of a happy evening. But it's specially nice to have somebody remind me of something even happier than the bouquets, the balloons, and the bubbly, something that will last out the day, the week, even the coming year, if there is any such thing. There is, you know. Here's joy:

> The wretched and the poor look for water and find none,
> their tongues are parched with thirst;
> but I the LORD will give them an answer,
> I, the God of Israel, will not forsake them.
>
> I will open rivers among the sand-dunes and wells in the
> valleys;
> I will turn the wilderness into pools
> and dry land into springs of water;

I will plant cedars in the waste,
and acacia and myrtle and wild olive;
the pine shall grow on the barren heath.

Isaiah 41:17–19 NEB

A birthday is a milestone. It's a place to pause. Look back now for a minute over the way the Lord has brought you. There has been thirst, hasn't there? You've been over some sand dunes, through some valleys, some wilderness, out on a barren heath once in a while. I have too. Sometimes it seemed that there weren't any rivers, wells, pools, or springs. Nothing but sand. No lovely acacias or wild olives, only barrenness. The trouble was I hadn't learned to find them. I was trying to travel alone. I made the same mistake when I first went to live as a missionary in the South American jungle. After one bad experience of getting lost, I learned to follow an Indian guide. He knew the trails. He could find water to drink (inside a bamboo, for example, if there wasn't a river handy), honey in a hollow tree, fruit where there seemed to be no fruit. I couldn't see them. I didn't know where to look. The Indian did. He could make a cup out of a palm leaf, build a fire in the rain, construct a shelter for the night in an hour or so. I was helpless. He was my helper.

A milestone is not only a place to look back to where you've come from. It's a place to look forward to where you're going. We don't always want to do that on birthdays. If we look back, it seems such a long time, the good old days are over, and (here's the hard part) so much guilt clogs the memories. If we look forward—alas. How many more birthdays? What will happen before the next one? Thoughts of the future are full of fear.

I, the LORD your God,
take you by the right hand;
I say to you, Do not fear;
it is I who help you.

Isaiah 41:13 NEB

39

Parties and presents won't do much for a checkered past or a frightening future. Only the God who was loving you then, loves you today on your birthday, and will keep right on loving you till you see him face-to-face can possibly do anything about them. "It is I who help you," he says. There is help for all the guilt. Confess it in full. He'll forgive it in full. And I mean *forgive*. That doesn't mean he denies its reality, sweeps it under the rug, or bathes it in sentiment. There was once an old rugged cross. You know where it was—on a hill far away. And you know what it means—nothing sentimental at all, but forgiveness, freely offered to all of us, the whole price paid in blood by the Dearest and Best.

There is help for your fear too. Express it in full. Let the Lord take you by your right hand and help you. I had to do that with my Indian guide. I simply could not make it across those slippery log bridges, laid high over jungle ravines, without help. I was scared to death. The Indian, who had been over them many more times than I had, held me by the hand.

You've heard those bad news/good news jokes. Well, this isn't cheap birthday card humor. The bad news is that another year has gone by and we haven't done all we meant to do and it's not going to come back to give us another chance. The good news is the gospel. We can be reconciled to God—sins forgiven, fears taken care of. That old cross, the emblem of suffering and shame, stands between us and our sins and fears, our past and future, and on its outstretched arms we see Love. The Love that would die for us is the Love that lives for us—Jesus Christ, Lord, Master, Savior of the world, wanting to give you (for your birthday if you'll take it) something that will really quench your thirst, rivers among the sand dunes and wells in the valley; wanting to hold your hand, help you, give you—not only a happy birthday, but everlasting joy.

I'm not the least bit bashful about telling my age. I'm glad for every birthday that comes, because it is the Lord, my faithful Guide, who "summoned the generations from the beginning." I look in the mirror and see the increasingly (and creasingly) visible proofs of the number of years, but I'm reconciled. Christ reconciles me to God and to God's wonderful plan. My life is his life. My years are his years. To me life *is* Christ, and death is nothing but gain. When I remember that, I really can't think of a thing I ought to be afraid of. I can't be sorry I'm a year older and nearer to absolute bliss.

I pray for you on your birthday, that your path, as is promised to the just man, will shine not less and less but more and more; that you will still bring forth fruit in old age; that the Lord will give you a thankful heart like the psalmist's who sang,

> O God, thou hast taught me from boyhood,
> all my life I have proclaimed thy marvellous works:
> and now that I am old and my hairs are gray, forsake me
>   not, O God. . . .
> Songs of joy shall be on my lips;
> I will sing thee psalms, because thou hast redeemed me.
> All day long my tongue shall tell of thy righteousness.
>
> Psalm 71:17–18, 23–24 NEB

So—happy birthday! If you have friends and parties and presents, be thankful for such bonuses. If you have no friends with you today, no party, not a package to open, you still have a long list of things to thank God for, things that matter much more. A birthday filled with thanksgiving and hope is the happiest kind of birthday. Have one of those! Deck yourself with joy!

6

I Won't Bother with a Face-Lift

Because tomorrow I will begin the last of threescore years, and because my mother is now closer to ninety than to eighty, I do a lot of thinking about old age. Has any of my friends called me "spry" yet, or remarked, "She's amazing—still got all her faculties"?

If they have, of course, it means they see me as over the hill, i.e., *old*. When I look in the mirror, I have to admit the evidence is all on their side, but otherwise it's hard to remember. I *feel* as "spry" and energetic as I did twoscore years ago.

I don't mind getting old. Before the day began this morning I was looking out at starlight on a still, wintry sea. A little song we used to sing at camp came to mind—"Just one day nearer Home." That idea thrills me. I can understand why people who have nothing much to look forward to try frantically and futilely to hang on to the past—to youth and all that. Get a face-lift, plaster the makeup on ever more thickly (but Estee Lauder says false eyelashes can add ten years to your looks), wear running shoes and sweat suits, dye your hair—anything to create the illusion you're *young*. (The illusion is yours, of course, nobody else's.)

Let's be honest. Old age entails suffering. I'm acutely aware of this now as I watch my mother, once so alive and alert and quick, now so quiet and confused and slow. She suffers. We who love her suffer. We see the "preview of coming attractions," ourselves in her shoes, and ponder what this interval means in terms of the glory of God in an old woman.

It would be terrifying if it weren't for something that ought to make the Christian's attitude toward aging utterly distinct from all the rest. *We know it is not for nothing.* "God has allowed us to know the secret of his plan: he purposes in his sovereign will that all human history shall be consummated in Christ, that everything that exists in heaven or earth shall find its perfection and fulfillment in him" (Eph. 1:9–10 Phillips).

In the meantime, we look at what's happening—limitations of hearing, seeing, moving, digesting, remembering; distortions of countenance, figure, and perspective. If that's all we could see, we'd certainly want a face-lift or something.

But we're on a pilgrim road. It's rough and steep, and it winds uphill to the very end. We can lift up our eyes and see the unseen: a Celestial City, a light, a welcome, and an ineffable Face. We shall behold him. We shall be like him. And that makes a difference in how we go about aging.

Why Funerals Matter

When a dear friend died recently, I found myself unexplainably disappointed when I learned that there would be only a memorial service. I wanted a funeral, and I was not sure why. Even more unexplainably, I wished there had been a "viewing" or wake—a chance to see her face. Is this wholly indefensible? I am sure that it is wholly human, but is it mere idle curiosity? Is it crass, or childish, or pagan, or materialistic? Is it hideously ghoulish?

"Christians do not need to make much of the body. We believe in the resurrection. We know the person is not here but There." Thus I argued with myself.

"Who wants to see somebody dead? Wouldn't you rather remember him as you knew him, strong and healthy and alive?" That makes sense too.

"Funerals are meaningless ordeals, pompous, expensive, emotionally costly, and serve no purpose other than conventional and commercial. And as for viewings—what can possibly be the point of coifing, painting, powdering, and dressing up a corpse, stretching it out lugubriously in a satin-lined mahogany box with its head on a fancy pillow, for people to stare at?" What indeed?

I could not come up with immediate rejoinders. There did not seem much logic in my protest. Didn't it spring from emotions alone, and those perhaps crude and primeval? Yes, very likely. But crude and primeval emotions may be eminently human and not necessarily sinful. They may even be useful. How do we know? Well, back to the Bible. What does it say?

The Bible does not say, "Thou shalt have funerals," or "Thou shalt not have memorial services."

When Jacob died there was the final scene in which he blessed each of his sons, then drew up his feet into the bed, breathed his last, and was "gathered to his people." Then Joseph threw himself on his father's body and wept over him and kissed him and commanded that he be embalmed. The Egyptians went through the customary seventy days of mourning. Then Joseph carried the body to Canaan, accompanied by a huge retinue of servants, elders, relatives, friends, chariots, and horsemen. Seven more days were spent in "a very great and sorrowful lamentation."

When Moses died God buried him, but the people of Israel wept for him thirty days. Joseph's bones were carried by the people of Egypt to be buried at Shechem.

Stephen was the first martyr, stoned to death, and it says "devout men buried Stephen and made great lamentation over him." It was right and proper that a man killed for his Christian witness should be buried by those who shared his faith—devout men. It was right and proper that they should grieve greatly, that they should grieve together, and that they should grieve "over him," which I take to mean literally over the grave.

Only last week my friend Van found her little black dog which had been lost ten days before. But she was dead—drowned in a pond where she had apparently fallen through the ice. Little Nell was Van's friend, and Van grieved for her, but she thanked God she found her and knew at last what had become of her. She lifted the wet furry thing in her arms and looked into her face and talked to her. Then, of course, giving her back to death, she buried her.

That was what we had been deprived of in my late friend's decision not to have a funeral. The memorial service was held eleven days after her death, and when we entered the church, there was nothing of her there. It would only have been a body, of course—but it would have been the "earthly house of this tabernacle" in which our friend had lived, through which we had known her, and it would have been the resurrectible body. It was long since deposited miles away in a mausoleum. We could not see her face. We could not even see a closed box with the knowledge that what was left of her was inside it. She had died of that most feared of diseases and no doubt its ravages were great. She had not wanted any of us to come near her during the last four or five weeks of her life. We understood her feeling. It is doubtful that she was in a position to understand ours. It was too late. I write this so that thoughtful people can consider the matter before it is too late.

We longed for the privilege of entering into her suffering insofar as it would have been possible. She was too ill to talk. We understood that. We would not have asked her to. If we had been allowed only to slip into the room for a minute, hold her hand, pray briefly or be silent, we would have been grateful. Perhaps a little of the loneliness of dying would have been assuaged for her, and a little of our sorrow and love communicated. I am sure that we, at least, would have been helped. But it was not to be. Even after she died, we to whom she had meant so much needed to establish a last link. That, too, was denied.

Several months ago a friend from New York wrote of the death of a child she had been close to. "I have mixed feelings about private funerals. Does that seem harsh to you? I so badly wanted to be with them in their grief, and I think a lot of others felt the same way. It was almost more than I could do, having an errand at the church, to walk past the hearse and out of sight before the family arrived. There will be a memorial service, but not for several weeks. I guess I am very old-fashioned or something. It is not a morbid hankering to 'view' the body, but the sight of a coffin brings home the reality and gives an outlet for grief, in my experience, as nothing else can."

Yes, my heart said, she is right. Now, after many years, I have sorted out why it mattered to me that we had only a memorial service for my first husband and real funeral for the second. In the first case, we had no choice. He was murdered, and the body was not found for five days. It was deep in uninhabited jungle from which transportation would have been nearly impossible. My second husband knew he was going to die, and we had time to discuss the funeral together. I don't remember his saying anything about a viewing, but I made that decision without difficulty as soon as he died. I knew that I had missed something when Jim died. Add had been beaten down by cancer, and the last weeks were horrifying. Somehow it was a relief to see his face one more time in a different setting from his sickroom. The face was thin and aged and pallid, of course, but this time free from pain. The strength of the features was still there, the brow, as somebody observed, still noble. I could say good-bye to him then in my heart and resign him to the grave.

When I was nine years old, my best and almost my only friend died. I remember the hot July day when I was playing in the side yard and my mother came out to tell me that Essie had gone. I remember my parents driving me up Broad Street in Philadelphia to the funeral parlor where she lay in a white dress with her golden curls around her face. She was nine years old too.

Nobody said to me, "But it's only a body. The spirit has flown, you know." Nobody needed to. I could see that. But I could also see my friend who had led me on many a wild chase through vacant lots and back alleys and had scared the wits out of me with terrible tales of giants she had run across. She was very quiet now, very subdued. My playmate was dead. The sight was very real to me. It was not a shock. Children are not shocked at things. It is their elders who cannot face reality. I was awed and solemn, and I thought about it for years afterward. It was a very wise decision of my parents to take me to the funeral.

I appeal to Christians. Plan your funeral now. If you are "getting on in years" it may be possible even to choose the minister and discuss things with him. If death seems more remote, at least write down the fact that you want a funeral, and choose hymns and Scripture passages to be used. Don't be too dogmatic about the practical arrangements. Leave those to whoever is responsible for disposing of you, so that it will be easiest for them.

But please remember your friends. They are the people to whom it will matter greatly to be allowed to bid you farewell, and to grieve in company with others who love you. Don't make light of that.

C. S. Lewis, that wise man who seems to have thought through almost everything, writes in his *Preface to Paradise Lost*: "Those who dislike ritual in general—ritual in any way and every department of life—may be asked most earnestly to reconsider the question. It is a pattern imposed on the mere flux of our feelings by reason and will, which renders pleasures less fugitive and griefs more endurable, which hands over to the power of wise custom the task (to which the individual and his moods are so inadequate) of being festive or sober, gay or reverent, when we choose to be, and not at the bidding of chance" (Oxford University Press, 1952, p. 21).

If it is a Christian funeral, we will be reminded in word and hymn that we do not "grieve like the rest of men, who have no hope. We believe that Jesus died and rose again; and so it will be for those who died as Christians; God will bring them to life with Jesus," and "we who are left alive shall join them, caught up in clouds to meet the Lord in the air" (1 Thess. 4:13–14, 17 NEB). Let funerals be, then, for Christians, celebrations in the presence of the mortal remains, visible signs of those glorious invisible realities which we believe with all our hearts.

Hope for a Hopeless Failure

Olive trees are not much good for leaning against. Too knobby. I kick away a few stones and sit down on the ground, knees braced in my arms. The other two stand for a while, eyeing the ones who had gone off alone.

"Might as well sit down," I say. They don't answer.

Long day. Tired. I look up through the trees. Ragged clouds, thin moon. Enough wind to move the olive leaves. My head's too heavy to hold up. I stare at my old sandals, one of them with a loose thong. Then I notice my feet and remember—at supper—"altogether clean." Dusty again now, but they were clean, all right. Never had them so clean. "Do you understand what I have done for you?" he asked. Maybe the rest understood. Not me. And what was all that about being *slaves*?

My two friends sit down a little way off. Can't hear much of the conversation (they're almost whispering). His body. His blood. (Strange things he said to us tonight at the table.) How he longed to eat with us, but would never do it again—until . . . something about a *kingdom*.

Yawn. Too tired to think now. I push away a few more stones and lie down in the grass. No pillow. Well, my arm will have to do.

What do I hear? Not my friends—they're flat out on the ground now, like me. Some movement. Wind? An animal? No, over *there*, where *he* is. A sort of gasp, was it? I strain my ears. Can't tell. Maybe they can, they're nearer, but they don't say anything. Silence now. Never mind. Have a little snooze.

"Asleep, Simon?"

I jump. He did ask us to stay awake, now that I think of it. He's standing over us and here we all are, snoring away. Poor show. "Pray that you may be spared the test." Yes, Lord. (Test?)

He goes off again. We sit up, shake ourselves. (It's colder now, my tunic's clammy with dew.) We pray. We can see, from the silhouette over by the rock, that something is very wrong. Wonder if we should do something? But he said stay here.

"You will all fall from your faith." We talk about that. What could he mean? *All* of us? The other two lie down. I sit here, thinking of what he said to me—about Satan, sifting me like wheat. He said he prayed especially for me. My faith fail? I told him I'd even go to prison with him. Die, if it came to that. Judas now—that's another story. Wonder what he's up to? Left the table in an awful hurry. Never did trust him. Shifty-eyed. Slick.

Uh-oh. Must have fallen asleep again. I can sense his presence, standing close, but I'll keep my eyes shut. What can I say? I wait. He says nothing, goes away.

"You awake?" I poke the others. I remember he told me I was to "lend strength to the brothers." They pull themselves up, and again we talk. He said he was going away. Somewhere where we could not come. Peace . . . love . . . the Prince of this world . . . persecution . . . the breakdown of faith. Doesn't sound good.

"What's that?" (I'm the one who's whispering now.) A soft noise—like wings. There's somebody there, bending over him in the moonlight. We peer through the trees. Can't tell who

51

it is. It's not good, his being here in this garden. Too many people know they can find him here. What! Whoever was there has—why, vanished! Just like that! He is standing now, his face lifted up.

"That's the third time he's prayed the same prayer," my friend says. I didn't hear it.

We keep talking, trying to stay awake this time. He needs me, I guess. We'd better be on our toes. Not sure what's going on. Is he in danger? But he doesn't seem to know fear. Has his own ways of getting out of trouble when he wants to—remember the time he slipped through the crowd that was about to dump him over the precipice? Yes, but we told him this time he ought not to come up to the city. Bad timing.

What about what he said about our needing purse, pack, and sword now, after sending us out *barefoot*, without a *coin* or a *crust*, the first time? Said he had a good many other things he couldn't tell us now, but would send a spirit—Spirit of Truth, that was it—who would explain things that were going to happen.

Hours go by. We lose track of how long we talk. Yawn, relax.

"Still sleeping? Up, let's go forward." On our feet like a shot. What's happening? "My betrayer is upon us." Mob surging through the garden. Lanterns, torches, swords, cudgels.

"Master! Here, quickly, get behind. . . ." He doesn't hear me. Walks straight up to them. "What is it you want?" I grab my sword, swing it at one of the gang, only get his ear.

"Put up your sword," he tells me. "This is the cup the Father has given me. Don't you realize I must drink it?"

What could we do? I follow him partway, but I can see it's all over. No point getting involved.

Years have passed now. The memory of what happened during the rest of that night is still sharp. A very dark night it was. But could I know what I know now, could I write things I write in my letters, if it had not happened?

Praise be to the God and Father of our Lord Jesus Christ, who in his great mercy gave us new birth into a living hope by the resurrection of Jesus Christ from the dead! The inheritance to which we are born is one that nothing can destroy or spoil or wither. It is kept for you in heaven, and you, because you put your faith in God, are under the protection of his power.

1 Peter 1:3–5 NEB

I know that mercy. I've been given that new birth. A hopeless failure, I know that living hope. No one deserved them less than I. No one can be more grateful than I, to whom so much was forgiven. Where would I be if he had not risen?

9

O Little Town of Nazareth

There is a town in Galilee called Nazareth. Years ago I passed through it very briefly at about noon on a chilly day in November. It seemed a dull place on the surface but far from dull to me as I thought of the stunning happening in one of its dull little houses one day nearly two millennia ago. The written account is excessively spare.

"The angel Gabriel was sent from God to a town in Galilee called Nazareth." A simple declarative sentence. Nothing superfluous, no superlatives. No lights, no sound effects, no advance publicity of coming attractions. An angel made a journey—think of it—"from God to a town." The fact is put (for us anyway) in words of one syllable.

Who was this angel? Not just any angel, but one with a name: Gabriel. We have met him before. About five hundred years earlier, in the first year of the reign of Darius, King of the Chaldeans, Gabriel had been sent to a man named Daniel. The divine Author of Scripture, who is also the divine Commissioner, pinpointed the precise place, the specific man, the exact era of human history and, most incredibly, the time of day. Daniel was praying, at the hour of evening sacrifice, when Gabriel came close to him, "flying swiftly."

How swiftly? Amy Carmichael, later to become a renowned missionary to India and author of dozens of books, recorded a conversation she had in 1887 with the Reverend James Gall, who imagined Gabriel's journey earthwards as taking

perhaps six, certainly not more than ten hours. In the first hour he would have left behind him the firmament of his native world, and entered the great wilderness of the universe, where no single star was visible, and where the black vault above, beneath, around was sprinkled only with its distant nebulae. He is alone with God, and, probably, in the solemn silence of his solitary flight, is receiving upon his inmost spirit the prophetic message that he was to bear to earth.

For hours together the same dread grandeur of nebulous scenery would continue, and yet the inconceivable swiftness of his progress would produce, as it were, a moving panorama around him.

To the close of his voyage, his course is directed to one particular nebula. It is our Milky Way, although as yet, it is no more than a mere speck in the distant night. Having entered the firmament of the Milky Way his eye is now directed to a feeble undistinguished star, upon which all his intent is concentrated. On he flies, passing Sirius, brighter than all beside, Orion, with his cloudy sword, the Pleiades, that vast system of congregated suns around which our own appears to be revolving, the Southern Cross, Neptune, Uranus, Saturn, Jupiter, Mars—on and on swifter than the light flies the "Pilgrim Angel" till at last he lays his hand upon the prostrate Daniel. It is the time of the evening oblations.

Mere speculation? But then, what was his route, if not on this wise? "But angels are ministering *spirits*," you say, "they need not travel physically, as we do." Perhaps not. But at some point Gabriel had to become aware of the physical. Was it when he entered the universe, or only when he entered the poor stone house? Such was his journey, I believe, to our planet when he was assigned to go to Nazareth. Unerringly he found the little dull town, the dusty street, the right house. In obedience he went in, stood before the astonished girl, and spoke—*in her own language.* "Greetings, most favored one! The Lord is with you." She is "deeply troubled." She wonders what this strange greeting means. The angel looks into her face, understands what is in her heart, and—can we try to imagine the sound of his voice? An angel's voice, speaking in the accents of Nazareth, speaking quietly, I suppose, for Mary's parents were no doubt nearby. Surely he speaks also tenderly to the frightened girl. "Do not be afraid, Mary [he knows her *name!*], for God has been gracious to you; you shall conceive and bear a son, and you shall give him the name Jesus . . . Son of the Most High . . . King over Israel forever . . . Son of God. God's promises can never fail."

Mary was not a feeble girl, weak and without spunk, imagination, or initiative. Subsequent action proves that. But she was meek. Never confuse weak with meek. She was meek as Moses was meek—strong enough and holy enough to recognize her place under God. Thoughts of what people would say, what Joseph her fiancé would say, or how she would ever convince them that she had not been unfaithful were instantly set aside. "Here I am, the Lord's handmaid," she said. "I will accept whatever he gives me."

Mission accomplished. The angel left her, the account says. Back he flies, past Mars, Jupiter, Saturn, Uranus, beyond the Southern Cross and the Milky Way into the black vault which Mr. Gall conceived as starless, and finally to the firmament of his native world where the will of the God of all those heavens and firmaments is always done, and always done perfectly.

Gabriel, too, had obeyed. He delivered the message. He brought back a message: on that planet, in Galilee, in a town called Nazareth, in the house to which God had sent him, the girl named Mary had said yes.

I cannot tell why He whom angels worship
should set His love upon the sons of men. . . .
But this I know; that He was born of Mary.

W. Y. Fullerton, *Keswick Hymnal*
Marshall, Morgan, and Scott

10

A No-Risk Life

The risks people are prepared to take these days are certainly a different set from what they used to be. I have been reading what Dickens and Kipling said about travel in their times. The reason I have been reading Dickens and Kipling just now when I am also trying to catch up with Solzhenitsyn and C. S. Lewis (I never catch up with Lewis—I have to start over as soon as I've finished one of his books because while I am always completely convinced by his argument, I find I can't reproduce it for somebody else, so I have to go back) is that a friend asked me to take care of some books she had just inherited from a rich aunt.

But it was risks I started out to write about. Dickens describes a journey into the Scottish Highlands:

> When we got safely to the opposite bank, there came riding up a wild highlander, his great plaid streaming in the wind, screeching in Gaelic to the post-boy on the opposite bank, making the most frantic gestures. . . . The boy, horses and carriage were plunging in the water, which left only the horses'

58

heads and boy's body visible. . . . The man was perfectly fran-
tic with pantomime. . . . The carriage went round and round
like a great stone, the boy was pale as death, the horses were
struggling and splashing and snorting like sea animals, and
we were all roaring to the driver to throw himself off and
let them and the coach go to the devil, when suddenly it all
came right (having got into shallow water) and, all tumbling
and dripping and jogging from side to side, they climbed up
to the dry land.

Kipling, in a speech made more than sixty years ago to the
Royal Geographic Society, looks forward to the possibilities
of air travel:

Presently—very presently—we shall come back and convert
two hundred miles across any part of the Earth into its stan-
dardized time equivalent, precisely as we convert five miles with
infantry in column, ten with cavalry on the march, twelve in
a Cape cart [which I found is a strong, two-wheeled carriage
used in South Africa], or fifty in a car—that is to say, into two
hours. And whether there be one desert or a dozen mountain
ranges in that two hundred miles will not affect our timetable
by five minutes.

Traveling nowadays means what it has always meant: facing
risks. Take air travel, for example. There is of course the total
risk—a crash—but most of us, when it comes to actually getting on a plane, are not preoccupied with that possibility. We
are much more conscious of the sort of risk that calls forth no
very high courage. Weather, topography, sources of food and
water along the way hardly concern us at all. We expect the
aircraft itself, the radar, the pilots, the mechanics, the caterers,
and the stewardesses to do their jobs, and we forget about them
from the start. We worry instead about whether we will get
stuck in the middle seat between two (perhaps fat) people who
use both arms of their seats, whether we'll have legroom after
we've stuffed our bag underneath the seat in front of us, and

whether a talkative seatmate will ruin our plans to get some serious reading done on a coast-to-coast flight.

There is a white paper bag in the seat pocket reminding us of another risk, "motion discomfort," which has superseded what sounds like a worse one, airsickness. The stewardess's voice comes over the intercom at takeoff, while another stewardess goes through a pantomime, telling us where to find the emergency exits and what to do in "the extremely unlikely event of a change in cabin pressure," and we pay no attention.

The apostle Paul was shipwrecked three times. He had to spend twenty-fours hours in the open sea. He wrote to the Corinthians:

> In my travels I have been in constant danger from rivers and floods, from bandits, from my own countrymen and from pagans. I have faced danger in city streets, danger in the desert, danger on the high seas, danger among false Christians. I have known exhaustion, pain, long vigils, hunger and thirst, doing without meals, cold and lack of clothing.

Well, Paul, once in a transoceanic flight in something called a jumbo jet, my daughter watched a movie for a whole hour before she realized that the sound track she had plugged into her ears was for another movie. (What do I mean by "flight"? "Movie"? "Sound track"? Never mind. They're all of them hazards you never had to cope with.) On top of that, the reading lights didn't work, there was no soap in the lavatories, no pillows or blankets on board although the air-conditioning was functioning only too well, and they served dinner at eleven o'clock at night and breakfast at one in the morning.

We take risks, all right. But what acquaintance have we with the physical hardships which used to be the testing ground for a man's character and stamina? We know nothing of the necessity of covering ground with our own two feet for days or weeks or months at a time, every step of which must be retraced on those same two feet if we're ever to get back to civilization again. We haven't felt the panic of isolation beyond help. When a book like *Alive: The Story of the Andes Survivors* appears, it becomes a best seller, for we recognize then the hermetic seal of our civilization.

An ancient longing for danger, for challenge, and for sacrifice stirs in us—us who have insulated ourselves from weather by heating and air-conditioning and waterproofing and Thermopane; from bugs, germs, pests, and odors by screening, repellents, insecticides, weed killers, disinfectants, and deodorizers; from poverty by insurance, Medicare, and Social Security; from theft by banks, locks, Mace, and burglar alarms; from having to watch others suffer by putting them where somebody else will do the watching; and from guilt by calling any old immorality a "new morality" or by joining a group that encourages everybody to do whatever feels good.

We don't risk involvement if we can help it. We try not to turn around if anybody screams. Responsibility for others we'd rather delegate to institutions, including the government, which are supposed to make it their business to handle it.

I saw a man on television just a few days after Mr. Ford became President telling us that what America needs is a little more honesty. Because of technology, the man said, people have to be more dependent on each other than they used to be (Oh?) and therefore we need more honesty (Oh). Probably, he allowed, our standards have never been quite what they ought to be, and it's time to hike them up a notch or two.

How do we go about this? Take a deep breath and—all together now—start being honest? Ah, the man had a plan. I waited, tense and eager, to hear what it might be. Popularization was what he proposed. Make honesty the In Thing. If everybody's doing it, it will be easy. In fact, the bright-eyed man told us, it would take the *risk* out of it.

Funny, I always thought righteousness was supposed to be risky. I was taught it wasn't easy, and I found it hard when I tried it. It's never likely to be either easy or popular.

"But I'm not asking for a change in human nature or anything," the man on the TV insisted, "only a change in attitude." And the round-eyed artlessness with which the remark was made and with which it was received by the TV host was breathtaking.

I'm for civilization. I'm all for certain kinds of progress, and I accept quite gladly most of today's means of avoiding the risks that Dickens and Kipling and all of humankind before them had to run, but to imagine that we shall whip off the dishonesty that is characteristic of fallen human nature everywhere as painlessly as we whip off one garment and put on another, to imagine that by simply taking a different view we shall come up with a no-risk brand of honesty, is a piece of self-deception and fatuity to make the mind reel.

Plato, three hundred years before Christ, predicted that if ever the truly good man were to appear, the man who would tell the truth, he would have his eyes gouged out and in the end be crucified.

That risk was once taken, in its fullest measure. The man appeared. He told the world the truth about itself and even made the preposterous claim "I am the Truth." As Plato foresaw, that man was crucified.

He calls us still to follow him, and the conditions are the same: "Let a man deny himself and take up his cross."

11

Shortcut to Peace

Later he said to Marjorie, "Brenda tried to be confidential about Beaver this evening."

"I didn't know you knew."

"Oh, I knew all right. But I wasn't going to let her feel important by talking about it."

Lines from Evelyn Waugh's *A Handful of Dust*

A Christian man who for many years has been helping alcoholics who want to be helped: "I make it clear from the start that I don't want to know where they've been. I've heard all that. I only want to know where they're going."

"She's been seeing a psychiatrist for months and says he's really fantastic, says she's just beginning to understand why she's been acting that way toward her husband."

"But does she really need to know all that?"

Most of us enjoy talking about ourselves, our problems, our escapades. We want to defend our mistakes ("I was really down that day") and explain our failures ("Couldn't get my head together"). People who are willing to listen make us feel important. Analysis not only exonerates us of full responsibility for bad behavior but even lends dignity. Sin, of course, is highly undignified. We dignify it by calling it something else. Trauma, hurts, "syndromes," and the whole pattern of ordinary human reaction to them are respectable. We would far rather discuss processes and symptoms than make the radical turnaround that means repentance. It is nicer to be soothed than summoned. As long as we are "undergoing treatment" or "in counseling," we can postpone decision.

I don't want to knock psychology, unless theology is being put at the *mercy* of psychology. That's dangerous.

Psychology may be a science, but it is certainly not an exact science. Psychiatry is even less exact, though it has risen almost to the place of supreme authority in our time. One theologian has called it "the anti-Christ of the twentieth century." I know one psychiatrist who has quit the field altogether and returned to general practice because, he says, "psychiatry does not exist. It is a pseudoscience."

Science at best is only science, and while we thank God for every realm of knowledge he has allowed people to enter, it is one thing to give it place. It is another to own its sovereign sway. Lewis Thomas, in an essay entitled "On Science and Uncertainty" (*Discover* magazine, October 1980), wrote, "It is likely that the twentieth century will be looked back at as the time when science provided the first close glimpse of the profundity of human ignorance. . . . Science is founded on uncertainty. . . . We are always, as it turns out, fundamentally in error. I cannot think of a single field in biology or medicine in which we can claim genuine understanding."

It would be good to keep Dr. Thomas's statement in mind when we are tempted to think that we shall, through psychological treatment or counseling, arrive at an understanding of ourselves which is deeper and closer to the truth than that which the writer of the book of Proverbs, for example, perceived.

When my father was editor of a religious weekly, a reader once wrote, "What is philosophy? Is it good or bad?" I have no record of his reply, but I suppose he told her it is a method of inquiry and in itself is neither good nor bad. Psychology is also a method of inquiry, but P. T. Forsyth said that it cannot go beyond method, has no machinery for testing reality, and has no jurisdiction in ultimates. In the sixty or seventy years since he wrote that, we have moved much closer to the edge of the precipice where we abandon the protection, restraint, and control of the everlasting Word and plunge over into the abyss of subjectivism. We need a control.

To change the metaphor: a certain psychological approach that seems to have gained tremendous popularity among Christians reminds me of the jungle rivers that I used occasionally to travel by canoe. They meandered. It was possible to get where you wanted to go by following the tortuous curves and loops, some of them almost doubling back on themselves. It was also possible to get there on foot by cutting straight through a curve, covering in ten minutes what it would take hours to cover by canoe.

To search out and sort out and "hang out" all the whys and wherefores of what we call our problems (a few of which just might be plain sins) may be one route to the healing of certain kinds of human difficulties, but I suggest that it may be the longest way home. I say this, I know, at the risk of being labeled simplistic, reductionist, obscurantist. But where, I want to know, does the *genuine understanding* that Dr. Thomas says science cannot claim begin? Where does it *begin*?

No man knows the way to it:

It is not found in the land of living men.
The depths of the ocean say, "It is not in us,"

and the sea says, "It is not with me."
Red gold cannot buy it,
nor can its price be weighed out in silver. . . .
Where then does wisdom come from,
and where is the source of understanding?
. . . God understands the way to it,
he alone knows its source.
And he said to man:
    The fear of the Lord is wisdom,
and to turn from evil is understanding.

Job 28:13–15, 23, 28 NEB

The ancient and tested source is revealed in a book whose re-
liability, relevance, and accuracy all fields of human knowledge
continue to corroborate. It is the Bible. My plea is not that we
reject the findings of psychology or any other field of study. It
is that we *start* instead with theology, with the knowledge of
God. Without that knowledge (given only to those who turn
from evil) there is "no jurisdiction in ultimates," no knowledge
even of ourselves, no certainty of any kind. My plea is that we
give the Word a first hearing, take our bearings there, and turn
only after that to whatever branch of science may apply to the
need in question. Chances are it will be a more direct route to
the truth, a shortcut to peace.

The Scriptures encompass the whole man, his whole world,
and reveal the Lord of the universe. In them we have not only
a perfect frame of reference, but specific and practical instruction, reproof when it's reproof we need, correction when we've
gone wrong.

I have found this to be true every time I have tried it.
Recently I was in turmoil about some things somebody said
to me. I lay awake at night, mentally enacting whole scenes
and conversations in which we would "have it out," dragging
everything into consciousness, saying everything that was in
our minds, pitting what she said against what I said, what she
did against what I did, defending and offending, complaining

and explaining. I had heard this was what we are supposed to do—get it out, get it up front, express it. But what a devastating business! What a crashing bore! What a way to consume time, not to mention emotional and spiritual energy! The very process itself gives me the chance to add to my own list of sins against her. "When men talk too much," says Proverbs 10:19, "sin is never far away; common sense holds its tongue" (NEB).

Psychology describes. The Bible prescribes. "Turn from evil. Let that be the medicine to keep you in health" (Prov. 3:7–8 NEB).

"Love is kind. Love is never quick to take offense. Love keeps no score of wrongs. There is nothing love cannot face; there is no limit to its faith, its hope, and its endurance" (1 Cor. 13:4–5, 7 NEB).

"Help one another to carry these heavy loads, and in this way you will fulfill the law of Christ" (Gal. 6:2 NEB).

"Let your bearing toward one another arise out of your life in Christ Jesus. . . . He made himself nothing . . . humbled himself . . . accepted death" (Phil. 2:5, 7–8 NEB).

The woman who had hurt me had plenty of heavy burdens to bear. I knew that very well. How could I help her to bear them? Well, for one thing, by "being offended without taking offense," that is, by following my Master.

What a relief! I no longer had to plot and plan and cogitate about how to handle my feelings or how to confront my friend or just what to say. My bearing toward her would arise *out of my life in Christ Jesus*. I couldn't do it myself. He could, and he would enable me.

To cut the straight path, a good deal of the jungle of my selfishness had to be slashed through. But it was a much shorter way home.

12

To Judge or Not to Judge

B ut everybody's being so judgmental! And you're another one," she complained. "Since you have chosen to be my judge, you can never be my friend."

For months Lisa had been watching Joan's behavior, which seemed to her to be very wrong. She had prayed about mentioning it. When she felt at last that she could no longer keep silent, she approached her dear friend in the spirit of Galatians 6:1–2:

> Even if a man should be detected in some sin, my brothers, the spiritual ones among you should quietly set him back on the right path, not with any feeling of superiority but being yourselves on guard against temptation. Carry each other's burdens and so live out the law of Christ (Phillips).

Joan, in response, was bitter, angry, and hurt. The wrong, she insisted, was Lisa's. Lisa was being "judgmental." The right, she felt, was on her side, for neither Lisa nor anyone else knew "the whole story."

The only verse about judgment in the Bible which anyone seems to have heard of these days is "Judge not." There the discussion usually ends. It is tacitly assumed that negative judgments are forbidden. That positive judgments would also come under the interdict escapes the notice of those who assume it is a sin to judge.

One morning long before dawn, I sat staring out onto a starlit sea, thinking of Joan and Lisa's story and of what Christian judgment ought to be. My thoughts ran like this:

If one does right and is judged to be right, he will be neither angry nor hurt. He may, if he is humble, be pleased (is it not right to be glad that right is done?), but he will not be proud.

If one who is proud does wrong and is judged to be wrong, he will be both angry and hurt.

If one who is proud does right and is judged to be wrong, he also will be both angry and hurt.

If one who is truly humble does wrong and is judged to be wrong, he will not resent it but will in gratitude and humility, no matter what it costs him, heed the judgment and repent.

If one who is truly humble does right and is judged to be wrong, he will not give the judgment a second thought. It is his Father's glory that matters to him, not his own. He will "rejoice and be exceeding glad," knowing for one thing that a great reward will be his, and, for another, that he thus enters in a measure into the suffering of Christ—"when he suffered he made no threats of revenge. He simply committed his cause to the One who judges fairly."

Joan was outraged that her close friend should judge her, thus disqualifying herself, Joan felt, from ever again being her friend. She failed to see that one as close as Lisa ought in fact to be the first to rebuke her, since she loves her and will be the first to notice that she needs to be rebuked. Joan, however, was sure that if Lisa could have seen the whole picture as God sees it, she would have judged differently: because what she was doing *was* right, both God and Lisa would see it to be right. That kind of "judgment" Joan would not have minded, nor would the word *judgmental* have entered her head. *Perceptive* or *discerning* are words which perhaps would have come to her mind.

Joan was right, of course, that Lisa did not see the whole picture. No one but God ever sees it, for only to him are all hearts open, all desires known. We mortals often fail to see right as right, wrong as wrong. We look on the outward appearance. It is all we have access to. We therefore know only in part.

In the meantime we are given the book of standards by which to judge our own actions and those of others. "By their fruits" we know them. If we were not to judge at all, we would have to expunge from our Christian vocabulary the word *is*, for whatever follows that word is a judgment: Jack is a fine yachtsman, Mrs. Smith is a cook, Harold is a bum. It depends on how one sees Jack, Mrs. Smith, and Harold.

Jesus told us to love our enemies. How are we to know who they are without judging? He spoke of dogs, swine, hypocrites, liars, as well as of friends, followers, rich men, the great and the small, the humble and the proud, "he who hears you and he who rejects you," old and new wineskins, the things of the world and the things of the Kingdom. To make any sense at all of his teachings requires, among other things, the God-given faculty of judgment, which includes discrimination.

The current popular notion that judging others is in itself a sin leads to such inappropriate maxims as "I'm OK and you're OK." It encourages a conspiracy of moral indifference that says, "If you never tell me that anything I'm doing is wrong,

I'll never tell you that anything you're doing is wrong." "Judge not that ye be not judged" has come to mean that if you never call anything sin, nobody can ever call you a sinner. You do your thing and let me do mine, and let's accept everybody and never mind what they're up to.

There is a serious misunderstanding here. The Bible is plain that we have no business trying to straighten out those who are not yet Christians. That's God's business. Alexander the coppersmith did Paul "much evil," and was "an obstinate opponent" of Paul's teaching. That description is a straightforward judgment, but Paul did not consider it his duty to deal with that man. "The Lord will reward him for what he did."

"But surely it is your business to judge those who are inside the church," he wrote to the Christians at Corinth, and commanded them to expel a certain immoral individual from the church:

> Clear out every bit of the old yeast. . . . "Don't mix with the immoral." I didn't mean, of course, that you were to have no contact at all with the immoral of this world, nor with any cheats or thieves or idolaters—for that would mean going out of the world altogether! But in this letter I tell you not to associate with any professing Christian who is known to be an impure man or a swindler, an idolater, a man with a foul tongue, a drunkard, or a thief. My instruction is: "Don't even eat with such a man."
>
> 1 Corinthians 5:7, 9–11 Phillips

That's pretty clear. And pretty hard to obey. I have seldom heard of its being obeyed in this country, but a missionary named Herbert Elliot tells me that he has seen it obeyed many times in the little Peruvian churches he visits in remote regions of the Andes and the jungle, where Christians simply believe the Word and put it into practice. In the majority of cases, he tells me, this measure has led to repentance, reconciliation, restoration, and healing.

71

The key to the matter of judgment is meekness. Childlikeness might be just as good a word. Meekness is one of the fruits of the Spirit. No one who does not humble himself and become like a little child is going to get into the Kingdom. We can never set ourselves up as judges, for we ourselves are sinners and inclined to be tempted exactly as those we judge are tempted. But if we are truly meek (caring not at all for self-image or reputation) we shall speak the truth as we see it (how else can a human being speak it?). We shall speak it in love, recognizing our own sinful capabilities and never-ending need for grace, as well as the limitations of our understanding. If we are to do the will of God in this matter, as in all other matters, we must do it by faith, taking the risk of being at times mistaken. We may misjudge, but let us be at least honest and charitable. We ourselves may be misjudged. Let us be charitable then, too, and accept it in humility as our Lord did. "When He was reviled, He reviled not in return."

I said we cannot set ourselves up as judges. It is God who sets us this task, who commands us Christians to judge other Christians. It is not pride that causes us to judge. It is pride that causes us to judge *as though* we ourselves are not bound by the same standards or tempted by the same sins. It was those who were trying to remove "specks" from a brother's eye when they themselves had "logs" in their own eyes to whom Jesus said, "Judge not."

"You fraud!" he said to them. "Take the plank out of your own eye first, and then you can see clearly enough to remove your brother's speck of dust." The dust must indeed be removed, not tolerated or ignored or called by a polite name. But it must be removed by somebody who can see—that is, the humble, the childlike, the pure, the meek. If any of us are inclined to excuse ourselves from the responsibility to judge, pleading that we do not belong in that lovely company, let us not forget that it is those of that company and only those who are of any use in the Kingdom, in fact, who will even enter it. We must take our stand with them beneath the cross of Jesus, where, as the hymn writer says:

... my eyes at times can see
The very dying form of One
Who suffered there for me.
And from my smitten heart, with tears,
Two wonders I confess:
The wonders of His glorious love,
And my own worthlessness.

Have It Your Way—or God's

When Lars and I lived in Georgia, he took me one Saturday night to a place called "Swampland" in the little country town of Toomsboro. It comprised a barnlike eating place and a barnlike auditorium where there was a gospel singing jamboree from four until midnight.

As we sat at a long table with a lot of people we didn't know, eating our catfish and hush puppies (there wasn't much else on the menu), we noticed an odd person standing by the fireplace. He was a kind of middle-aged hippie. He had long gray hair like a broom. He was wearing baggy patched pants, a jacket with fringes (some of them on purpose and some just tatters), a pistol belt, and a hat that was so greasy Lars said it would burn for a week if it ever caught fire. Every now and then he gave the logs on the fire a poke or two, but seemed to be otherwise unoccupied.

When the manager of the restaurant came by, table-hopping, we asked about the local character.

"You mean old Rusty Russell there? You don't know Rusty Russell?"

We said no. We asked if he was the official fire-poker.

"Nope."

"What does he do?"

"Do? Don't do nothin'. Come with the place." The manager went on to tell us a little more. Seems he was from Alabama originally. His old daddy used to live with him, and when he died, Rusty wanted to bury him back home in Alabama. Dressed him up in his Sunday suit, put a Sunday hat on his head, belted him into the front seat of his old Ford car, and headed out of town.

"Health authorities caught up with him, though. It was summertime. No way was they gonna let him drive that corpse outa state.

"Old Rusty had a wife once too. Next-door neighbor took a shine to 'er. Rusty goes over, says, 'See you like ma wife.'

"'Yup,' he says.

"'Want 'er?' Rusty says.

"'Yup,' he says.

"'What'll you give me for 'er?'

"'Stove,' he says.

"Old Rusty says, 'I'll take it.'

"He did. Traded his wife for a woodstove. Good one too. Rusty still uses that stove, by golly. Got a good deal. Better'n the neighbor got, I reckon."

We loved that story. We did not love the story we heard last week—three stories, in fact, depressingly familiar, of three ministers of the gospel who, like Rusty's neighbor, let their eyes wander to their neighbors' wives. All three liked what they saw next door (or, more accurately, in one of the pews of their churches) and, hearkening to current commercials ("You can have it all," "Do yourself a favor," "Have it your way") opted out.

Among the processes accelerating the breakdown of human structures is the flooding of imagery, produced by the mass media, "sweeping us into a chaotic and unassimilable whirlpool of influences," writes Dr. James Houston in *I Believe in the Creator* (Eerdmans, 1980). "We are overwhelmed by undigested data, with endlessly incomplete alternatives to every sphere of living."

Christians, encouraged by the example of Christian leaders everywhere, have begun to regard divorce as an option. There is nothing new about marital difficulties. If a man who is a sinner chooses as a life partner a woman who is a sinner, they will run into trouble of some sort; depend upon it. Paul was realistic about this in 1 Corinthians 7:28: "Those who marry will have worldly troubles, and I would spare you that" (RSV).

Jill Briscoe says that she and her husband Stuart are incompatible. She told a whole audience this. "And we live with incompatible children and an incompatible dog and an incompatible cat." The point she makes is: when it comes right down to it, aren't all human beings incompatible? It takes grace for any of them to get along on an every-day-of-the-year basis. The apostle Peter, who was married, reminded us that a husband and wife are "heirs together of the grace of life." God knows our frame, remembers that we're nothing but dust and that we need grace, lots of grace. This God supplies—plenteous, sufficient, enough—to those willing to receive.

If we receive that grace with thanksgiving, he will enable us to make the sacrifice of self without which no human relationship will work very well. The refusal of grace is like the refusal to put oil in an engine. The machinery will break down. Prolonged friction between the parts will result in the whole thing's grinding to a halt. When, for lack of grace in one or both partners, a marriage grinds to a halt, the "world," coming at us loud, clear, and without interruption via television and other media, persuades us that we have plenty of alternatives. The church, always in danger of pollution by the spirit of the world, begins to choose the proffered alternatives in preference to grace, to replace "I believe" with "I feel."

There is an eternal Word that has been spoken. For thousands of years Christians have taken their stand on that Word, have driven into it all the stakes of their faith and hope, believing it to be a liberating Word, a *saving* Word. They have arranged their lives within its clear and bounded context.

The trouble with television is that it has no context. We sit in our living rooms or stand, as I often do, dicing carrots in our kitchens with the Sony on the counter. The program comes to us from New York or Hollywood or Bydgoszcz or Virginia Beach. The set—a corner of an elegant living room, a city street, a desk high in some skyscraper, or perhaps Cypress Gardens or a "crystal" cathedral—seems fake even if it is real. It has nothing to do with us or with what is being spoken. There is no context which embraces both my life and theirs, or it is "the context of no-context," as George W. S. Trow argued brilliantly in a *New Yorker* article (November 17, 1980):

> The work of television is to establish false contexts and to chronicle the unraveling of existing contexts; finally to establish the context of no-context and to chronicle it. . . . The New History was the record of the expression of demographically significant preferences: the lunge of demography *here* as opposed to *there*. . . . Nothing was judged, only counted. The preferences of the child carried as much weight as the preferences of an adult, so the refining of preferences was subtracted from what it was necessary for a man to learn to do.

Divorce has become "demographically significant" among Christians. So have too many other things. It is because we have forgotten that our context is the Kingdom of God, not the kingdom of this world (which is the kingdom of self). In the Kingdom of God the alternatives are not boundless, not so long as we live in this mortal coil. You can't have it all. You are not there to do yourself a favor. You may not have it your way. You opted out of all that when you made up your mind to follow a Master who himself had relinquished all rights, all equality with the Father, and his own will as well. You are called not to be served but to serve, and you can't serve two masters. You can't operate in two opposing kingdoms. These kingdoms *are* the alternatives. Settle it once for all. It is, quite simply, a life-and-death choice. Pay no attention to what is demographically significant.

I receive a good many letters from young people who are utterly at sea about their life's choices—college, career, marriage. They are faced with too many alternatives. The seeming limitlessness overwhelms, unsettles, often even paralyzes them. (Can I have marriage *and* a career? Can I have marriage and a career *and* babies? Can I be really feminine and be an initiator? Can I be really a man and not the head of my home?) Twenty years ago they were faced with a whole cupboard full of packaged breakfast foods and were asked by a well-meaning but unwise mother what they wanted for breakfast. They didn't know. They have been going to McDonald's ever since, gobbling up those (how many billions is it now?) hamburgers with or without onion, with or without mustard, relish, catsup, everything. They still think they can have it all, and they still don't know what they want. Why not stop bothering about what *you* want, I suggest to them. Find out what your Master wants.

The three ministers think they know. They married the wrong woman. A youthful mistake. They've grown apart now. The children will not be hurt if they "handle" it properly, they say. They owe it to themselves to take this daring and creative step. God wants them to be happy. It's a leap and a risk and there's a price to pay, but look how liberating, how stretching, how redemptive. Why be threatened by traditional morality? Why be hung up? The other woman has understood and af- firmed and fulfilled them as the poor wife was never equipped to do and—a line from an old song reminds them—"to waste our lives would be a sin."

Twirl those television dials. Look, for a minute, at the suf- fering of the world on the evening news. Twirl it off. Look at the beautiful people if you want to. There they are. You can be beautiful too. You can do what they do, go where they go. TWA will take you up, up, and away. Delta is ready when you are. Become a legend. Charm a holiday party. Enhance your fragrance image. Give to thyself. Wear the Mark of Success. Try everything. Experience all the thrills.

Now it may be the flower for me
Is this beneath my nose,
But how shall I tell unless I smell
The Carthaginian rose?

So wrote Edna St. Vincent Millay (*Collected Lyrics*, Washington Square Press) decades ago. In the 1980s the possibilities seem even more endless and enticing, the unreached corners of the world ever more reachable, the pleasures of sin more innocuous. In fact, we suspect, they are not even luxuries. They have become, for the self-respecting man or woman, requirements.

There is plenty of room on the road that leads to that kingdom, and many go that way, but it is still true that the gate that leads to life is small and the road is narrow and those who find it are few.

Person or Thing?

Not long ago *Time* magazine reported another triumph of modern medical technology. An unborn child, found, by means of a process called amniocentesis, to suffer from Down's syndrome, was aborted (terminated? quietly done away with? killed?). It was all very safe and scientific and sterile. Not only was there little danger to the mother, there was no harm to the other twin in the mother's womb. The affected child (Is that an acceptable word? Should I say afflicted? unwanted? undesirable? useless? disposable?) was relieved of its life by being relieved of its lifeblood, which was slowly withdrawn through a long needle that pierced its beating heart. This was called a therapeutic abortion. The word *therapeutic* means serving to cure or heal. The strange part about this case was that nobody except the aborted child was ill. Who then was cured? Who was healed?

It seemed a huge irony that only a few weeks later the same magazine hailed another medical breakthrough: surgery to correct an abnormal kidney condition known as hydronephrosis. The amazing part about this case was that the patient was an unborn child, again one of twins. Again, a needle was inserted—through the mother's abdominal wall, through the uterus, through the amniotic sac lining, through the abdominal wall of the fetus, into the bladder. The needle was not used to withdraw blood but to insert a catheter that would drain urine, thus saving little Michael's life.

"For all its promise," *Time* commented, "fetal surgery poses some difficult ethical dilemmas."

Difficult indeed but only if we refuse to call the thing operated on a child.

In the first case, the mother did not want it. Whatever she called it, it had every possibility of becoming a person, and only as a person posed a threat. When it was rendered harmless, that is, when the heart no longer beat, when it was, in fact, dead, she continued to carry it to term. Then, along with its twin, it was born. Its twin had been very like itself to begin with, fully capable of becoming a person, but now very different indeed—wanted, desirable, "useful"—and alive.

In the second case, the mother wanted both the twins, the well one and the sick one with the swollen bladder and kidneys. To her, what was in her womb was her children. Could they possibly save the tiny thing? Was there anything they could do for her baby? It was (Did the mother ever question it?) a baby.

Dr. Leonie Watson said, "If they can do surgery on a fetus, then it is in fact a baby."

We recognize how far we have departed from what nature has always told any prospective mother, when we realize that *arguments* must be adduced, some of them even from technical procedures like fetal surgery, to prove that the living, moving creature about to come forth into the world is a human baby. *If* surgery is possible, *then* it's a baby.

This is, of course, where the battle lines are drawn. Is it, or is it not? What is the thing to be aborted? What is the thing to be born? What is the thing on which surgery was done?

If we call it a fetus, does it make the ethical dilemmas less difficult?

Dr. Phillip Stubblefield, a gynecologist at Boston's Massachusetts General Hospital, argues that a fetus is a baby only if it can live outside the womb.

If we can accept this assertion, may we also assume that a patient is not a person unless "it" can survive without, for example, dialysis or a heart pump? Is a machine somehow more humanizing than a womb? Is it possible seriously to believe that successful detachment from the mother is what turns an otherwise disposable and expendable mass of tissue into what we may legitimately call a baby?

Katharine Hepburn recently sent out a letter (I suppose to nearly everybody; otherwise I don't know how I would have gotten on her list) appealing for $3.6 million to stand up against what she called "repressive legislation" to limit individual rights and reproductive freedom. She listed eight reasons a certain amendment which would prevent abortion on demand should be defeated. Not a single one of her eight reasons would stand up in any court as a valid argument against the amendment *if* the thing aborted were called a person.

That is the question.

That is the only relevant question.

When what Miss Hepburn calls "individual rights and reproductive freedom" impinge on the rights of a person other than the pregnant woman, that is, on a person who happens to be hidden, helpless, and at the mercy of the one entrusted with his or her life, are we who object hysterical, illogical, bigoted, fanatic? Are we duped by what she calls "simple outdated platitudes of television preachers" if we cry aloud against her and her kind?

Last week there was another scandal. A woman had been running nursing homes that turned out to be what an investigator called "human sewers." She made a great deal of money off another group of defenseless human beings—the elderly, who had something in common with the "fetuses" Miss Hepburn claims the right to dispose of. They, too, were hidden, helpless, and at the mercy of the one entrusted with their lives. People were outraged. These victims had not been treated as human beings.

Why all the fuss? Suppose we apply some of the arguments used in favor of abortion to the treatment of the indigent, the friendless, the senile.

If there is brain damage or deformity, the fetus (read also the senile or the crippled) may be terminated.

If the fetus's becoming a person, i.e., being born, would be a serious inconvenience to the mother, or to other members of the family, it may be terminated. As has often been observed, there is no such thing as a "convenient" time to have a baby. All babies (and many disabled or bedridden people) are an inconvenience. All are at times what might be called a serious inconvenience. Love alone "endures all things."

If a baby is allowed to be born, he or she may become the victim of brutality. One solution offered for the "battered child syndrome" is abortion. What about the "neglected octogenarian syndrome?"

A sixteen-year-old high school student who has no prospect for a stable home and whose pregnancy will end her chance for an education is counseled to abort her baby. How shall we counsel a fifty-eight-year-old divorced man about what to do with his invalid mother? Taking care of her might end his chances for a lot of things.

If we refuse to allow medically "safe" abortions, we are told that we thereby encourage "back-alley butchery," self-induced procedures of desperate women, even suicide. By the same token, if we outlaw sterile injections of, say, an overdose of morphine administered to an elderly nursing home resident whose "quality of life" does not warrant continuation, do we thereby encourage less humane methods of getting people out of the way?

Miss Hepburn deplores "cold constitutional prohibitions," prefers instead individual choice based on "sound advice from the woman's personal physician." Some of those cold constitutional prohibitions happen to deal with the question of human life and what we citizens of these United States are allowed to do for or against it.

That is still the question. What do we do with the gift of life? Shall we acknowledge first of all its Creator, and recognize the sanctity of what is made in his image? Shall we hold it in reverence? If any human life, however frail, however incapable of retaliation, is entrusted to us, shall we nourish and cherish it, or may we—by some enormously civilized and educated rationalization—convince ourselves either that it is not a person, or that, although it is a person, its life is not worth living, and that therefore what we do with it is a matter of individual choice?

What *is* this thing?

We are faced with only one question. Are we talking about an object, or might it by any stretch of the imagination be a person? If we cannot be sure of the answer, at least we may pick up a clue or two from the word of the Lord that came to Jeremiah: "Before I formed you in the womb I knew you for my own; before you were born I consecrated you, I appointed you a prophet to the nations" (NEB). To God, at least, Jeremiah was already a person. For my part, I will try to regard whatever bears the marks of humanity as God's property and not mine.

15

To a Man Who Chose Divorce*

Dear Dick:

It was like a kick in the stomach to hear that you decided to get rid of Sally and the babies. We had heard some months ago that there was trouble. We did not know the nature or the seriousness of it, but we prayed. You opted for divorce and now it's all over. Or is it? You have your "freedom," such as it is, you live in the bachelor officers' quarters, and you can do what you like, without sacrifice or responsibility, while Sally is looking for a job and her parents have stepped in to help with the job you once promised to do—taking care of your wife and your babies.

I wrote to you, asking you to call, but no call came. I can understand why you did not want to talk to me or anyone else who might try to talk you out of what you had made up your mind to do. Your explanation for the decision, I am told, was that you did not want to be a husband, you did not want to be a father. As simple as that. But very poor timing, if I may say so.

*This and the following two chapters were never sent to anyone. They were written as a means of sorting through what I would say if a couple were to allow me the opportunity to counsel them while reconciliation was still possible.

"Wait a minute," you say. "You don't know the whole story." That's true. There is much on each side that I know nothing about. But I know this: you took a vow to cleave to Sally in sickness or in health, for richer, for poorer, for better *or for worse*, as long as you both should live. What did you think you meant by those words? A real man (that is, a true man) is always a man of his word.

You are a child of your generation. I can hear your answer: "But I've changed. Sally's changed. She's not the woman I married. I'm no longer the same man who mouthed those words (and they were only words, a tradition, a ceremony we went through to satisfy society). Things have happened to alter everything. Will you get off my back?"

You have grown up in a time when people are declaring their independence of what they choose to call "other people's morality." "What right do they have to tell me what to do? I have to do what's right for *me*," they whine, as though self-ishness may be destructive for one man and constructive for another, as though putting the happiness of another before your own really need not be a part of the marriage contract in the 1980s.

You have your freedom, I said a moment ago, but it is only a manner of speaking. There is no freedom anywhere in the universe apart from the freedom we were created for in the very beginning: to glorify God. I'm not telling you anything you have not grown up knowing. You know also that the choices in life resolve themselves ultimately to this one: God or self. You are searching for some place in God's world where you need not face so stark a choice. You will never find it.

You have supposed that you can elect to stop being a hus-band and father. It is like saying, "Stop the world, I want to get off," because the truth is that you and Sally became one flesh. Divorce papers do not undo that. You begat two sons. Abandoning them cannot nullify your fatherhood. Your chil-dren will always be yours, and they will always know that you discarded them. I have no idea what the legal arrangements are, whether you have "visiting rights" or whatever, but no matter. Those are nothing more than legal arrangements. The cold fact stands that you rejected the gift of fatherhood along with the gift of being husband and head and priest in the home you chose under God to establish.

"Sally can marry somebody else," you are quoted to have said. Perhaps she will. Your children will then have a stepfather who may love them as you ought to have loved them, and accept responsibility for their care, which you have shrugged off. No protests that you love them, that you do indeed want to see them from time to time and pay their bills, can ever change the fact that you quit. Things were tough, so you bugged out.

You are in the military service now, Dick. Things might get tough there too, but I would imagine you were sworn in. You pledged your word to serve, to obey the rules, to be loyal. Have we, the citizens of the United States, any reason to expect you to keep your word if you find, after a while, that you've changed, circumstances have changed, things were not exactly what you bargained for? Will you confront the difficulties by breaking the promises you swore to keep? Is your word to your country worth any more than your word to God or to the witnesses before whom you plighted your troth to Sally?

You are holding imaginary dialogues with those who condemn your action (people like me), proving that you had to do it, you couldn't take it any longer, it will turn out all right in the end, it will be much better for Sally and the boys. I hope you *are* holding such dialogues, because it would show that you needed to justify your action. Action that is clearly right needs no justification.

I dare to hope, too, that in some predawn hour of sleeplessness in your solitary bed, you have admitted that you have not found the freedom you were looking for. You face, in saner moments, the sad truth: you have been irrevocably changed by quitting. If you are half the man we thought you were, you are hating yourself for what you have done. The arguments you have adduced—you are being honest, you were living a lie

87

while you were married, you finally got in touch with your real feelings and summoned the courage to defy convention and the expectations of all who love you—are beginning to ring hollow. You know that the "real feelings" of all of us nearly all the time are selfish, and what we conveniently call convention might be (in this case *is*) the clear command of God: What God has joined together, man must not separate (Matt. 19:6 NEB).

I earnestly hope that you have not fallen so far as not to be ashamed of yourself.

"In trying to extirpate Shame," wrote C. S. Lewis, "we have broken down one of the ramparts of the human spirit, madly exulting in the work as the Trojans exulted when they broke their walls and pulled the Horse into Troy. I do not know that there is anything to be done but to set about rebuilding as soon as we can. It is mad work to remove hypocrisy by removing the temptation to hypocrisy: the 'frankness' of people sunk below shame is a very cheap frankness" (*The Problem of Pain*, p. 45).

What you have done is detestable. Understandable, of course, but detestable. I know that from the Book. It says, "God hates divorce." If we do not also hate it, we are not on God's side. I dare to hope that you still think of yourself as on his side and are therefore, at least when you are not paying attention to the enemy's suggestions, thoroughly ashamed. This is your hope of salvation. Until you accept God's estimate of the thing done, you will never seek his remedy.

Your present discontent is a mercy, affording opportunity to repent. Any inkling you have that all is not well is the still, small voice calling you back to repentance, reconciliation, and restoration. Will you set about rebuilding as soon as you can?

The "Innocent" Party

When a letter I wrote to a man who chose divorce was published, I heard from a reader who said it was unduly harsh and did not seem to have any love in it. "I can't picture Jesus saying such a thing to anyone," he wrote. "It implies that Dick was bad and Sally was good."

Let's examine this for a minute. The harshness, I suppose, is inferred first because I said the news of the divorce was "like a kick in the stomach"—in other words, it hurt me personally. Any divorce ought to be bad news to a Christian because we know how God feels about it. This particular divorce was terrible news to me because I happen to love both Dick and Sally. If my letter to Dick seemed to my correspondent to have no love in it, perhaps that was because he imagines that love and judgment are mutually exclusive. If you love people, you will never say anything that will make them uncomfortable.

I wonder how attentively he has read the Gospels. Jesus often made people uneasy. Sometimes he made them furious. I wonder, too, how attentively my correspondent has read the letters of Paul, Peter, and James. Those letters teach us clearly and strongly to call a thing what God calls it. If it's sin, call it sin. Deal with it as sin.

This goes for our own sins first, *of course*. We are judged by the Word. It is the straightedge that shows up our own crookedness. Let us confess our own sins, root them out, forsake them. Then, when we've done that (Jesus explained it vividly)—taken the "log" out of our own eye—we will be able to see well enough to take the "splinter" out of somebody else's. (Isn't it an act of kindness to take out a splinter for somebody?)

"Oh, come on, now—who do you think you are?" I hear someone saying. "What do you know about the situation between a husband and wife? You can't judge. Mind your own business!"

I said in my letter to Dick that there was much on both sides that I knew nothing about. I wrote to him solely about what I did know: he had made public vows, he had broken them. I hoped that there was still time to repent, to restore a relationship, to mend a shattered home and heal the appalling wounds of two little children.

But did I imply that Dick was bad and Sally was good? I did not. It is a very confused line of thought that says the guilt of one implies the innocence of the other. Let's assume that Sally was worse than Dick. He had promised to love and cherish her, for better or for worse. He broke that promise. That Dick sinned was clear enough, and I said so. I did not say that Sally had not sinned. The person sinned against is not necessarily innocent. Far from it. Given the propensities of human nature, the very fact that one is sinned against dramatically enlarges the ordinary field of temptation to sin. I had no way of knowing how Sally might have sinned, but I supposed she did. I supposed that, being a woman, she is something like me. Full of pride, I would be dumbfounded, then hurt, devastated, furious, and vindictive. I would feel extremely sorry for myself and would spend a good deal of time and emotional energy thinking of ways to retaliate, as well as to condemn Dick and justify myself. In other words, I could not possibly be called an innocent party.

Those are things I would be likely to have done when Dick told me he was leaving. The man who wrote to me suggested a list of things Sally might have done before and after his decision. "I challenge you," he wrote, "to write another letter to Sally about how she demanded things done her way, was often nasty and sarcastic, often used 'the good of the children' to get her way. How she used every trick to get her man hooked and then did not follow through. How she finally convinced Dick the children were better off without him than to be a constant source of quarrels. How she sort of liked being a heroine and making Dick look bad. How she had to build up her ego by being not only the nurturer of the children but the breadwinner as well. How she in her self-righteousness is going to bring up the children away from the bad influence of their dad."

Sally may be guilty of all these sins and more. Dick's list of offenses may be even longer. I do not know either side of the sad story. I am sure if I heard Sally's side my sympathies would be with her. If Dick told me his side the very next day, my sympathies would promptly shift to him. I would conclude that both were right and both were wrong, there was a lot to be said on both sides, and we might as well throw up our hands and say, "Do your own thing. There's no way to work this out." Dick went to a psychologist who called himself a Christian (they tell me), who spent his time, not encouraging Dick to love Sally in obedience to God and thus to avoid divorce, but helping him "deal with his feelings" when the divorce happened.

I do not, I admit, know the story. But I know the One who knows it—all of it—and I know that *it is always possible to do what he tells us.*

The actress Katharine Hepburn had little patience for actors who surrendered to "the tortuous introspection of the Method," *Time* says. "You do what the script tells you," she said. "Deliver the goods without comment. Live it—do it—or shut up. After all, the writer is what's important."

That goes for us Christians. There *is* a script. If there weren't, then we'd have to muddle through on our own, hoping by introspection and experiment to come up with something that might work. God hasn't left us to that method. He knew what we'd get into by sinning and has made provision for us. Let's live it—do it—or shut up and quit pretending to follow Christ. The issue we are discussing here is not whether Dick had good reason for unloading his family, but whether he had an option according to the Script. "We never discussed a script," said Hepburn, "we just did it. Naturally and unconsciously we joined into what I call a musical necessity." Easier, I suppose, in theater than in the confusion and pain of a real marriage, but there is a "musical necessity" for all of us. Even when we cannot solve our problems, we can please God. Even when one person disobeys him, the other can obey him. My husband Lars and I know this is true. Poor students though we are ("fools and slow of heart to believe") we're daily trying to do our lessons in the school of faith and obedience, finding the truth of the old gospel song, "There's no other way to be happy in Jesus."

There is a common assumption today that whatever we are and wherever we are is somehow fixed and inevitable, while it is the ancient Word that must be bent. For example, a woman cheats a university by plagiarizing and is refused a diploma. She decides she has a right to the university's credentials even though she happens to be a cheater, so she sues. Another woman chooses abortion. It is fixed and inevitable, in her mind, that what might turn into a baby must be got rid of, never mind the possibility that it's murder. People protested the Abscam experiment because, after all, nobody can be expected to resist *that* much money. To be loving, caring, sharing, and daring in the Christian community too often means, for example, to tell Dick he's okay, he's got his own life to live, and to tell Sally nobody can blame her for feeling sorry for herself.

"Blame"? The question here is who assigns blame? There is an ancient Word, fixed, settled, that shall stand forever. The present situation is only grass that withers and flowers that fade. We must quit bending the Word to suit our situation. It is *we* who must be bent to that Word, *our* necks that must bow under the yoke. Love is no pleasing sentiment but a fiery law: *thou shalt love.* In Dick and Sally's predicament, I can only imagine how deeply that fire will have to burn if they decide to obey. I can imagine it, all right, for I know the sinfulness of my own heart and how much dross is there to be purified by the Refining Fire, how excruciating it is for me to submit to the Word that never permits the least indulgence of self-pity, self-vindication, self-aggrandizement, self-justification, or any other form of the self whatsoever.

A young woman called me the other day to describe what seemed an utterly insoluble marital problem. My heart was entirely with her. She lives with a man who seems to me and to many others "impossible." The things he asks her to do are unreasonable and absurd.

"He wants me to do so-and-so, but I'm not going to do it." I had little to say in reply, except that I would keep on praying for them.

"I guess you'd call that a stalemate, wouldn't you?" she said.

I guessed I would. There was a pause. Then she said, "But Elisabeth, you know, I have a strong feeling that it will remain a stalemate unless *I* do something. I think God is asking me to make the move, to submit to Jack. Do you think that would be right?"

"Yes."

"I don't think I can do it. I just can't do it. I keep hoping God will make it easy for me . . . but I guess he's not going to, huh?"

"Often in the Bible we find God bringing people to a place of decision—often an 'impossible' decision (think of the Israelites in the Old Testament, the man with the withered hand in the New)—and at that point it's up to them. The refusal to obey when the choice is clear is the end of blessing," I said. "Obedience leads to some unimagined solution."

I knew how fearsome the choice was in her case. God knew it too. But God is the one who takes responsibility for the results when the choice is made in obedience. This is always the thing we can count on. Human relations present "impossible" difficulties. Sin seems to tie us into hopeless knots, and we seek desperate solutions: divorce, abortion, lawsuits. Of course, people understand. People sympathize. Some criticize, some judge as though they themselves would never be so tempted. This is wrong, and for me to say it is wrong is a *judgment*. But it is not my judgment. It is the judgment of the Bible. The Bible tells us it is wrong to judge—not wrong to use our critical faculties, but wrong to set ourselves up as righteous and immune to the sin we are judging. "Judge *righteous* judgment," Jesus said.

We have laid many traps for ourselves by forgetting how sinful we are and how badly we need the Script. We get into a mess and we declare ourselves bankrupt. Nobody can make any moral claims against us anymore. We are, spiritually speaking, out of business, closed. We're doing our thing, defying those who judge us, telling them it is always wrong to judge (which is in itself a judgment but not one based on the Script).

My correspondent told me we should remember we've all broken vows, that Dick was doing the best he could, and that I shouldn't make matters worse by making him feel bad, that I should love and care about him instead of criticizing so harshly. He said divorce was common in Bible times; it's better to separate than to live in hatred; and why don't we all just try to support the good and stop condemning the bad?

My correspondent was muddled. Trying to be humble and sensible and loving, I'm sure, but muddled nevertheless. Let's try to be clear. When sinful people live in the same world, and especially when they work in the same office or sleep in the same bed, they sin against each other. Troubles arise. Some of those troubles are very serious and not subject to easy solutions. God knows all about them and knew about them long before they happened. He made provision for them. His Son bore all of them—all grief, all sorrow, all disease, all sin—for us. But why on earth (or in heaven) should he have done that? Why "should" he? He shouldn't, but he did. Because of love. The love that is stronger than sin, stronger than death.

And here is the profound lesson for us in the midst of our troubles. To rescue us out of them, Christ relinquished his rights. Are we his followers? Then let's take a hard look at what we have a right to expect from others. What does Sally rightfully expect from Dick? Love. "Husbands, love your wives." What does Dick rightfully expect from Sally? Submission and respect. "Wives, be subject to your husbands as to the Lord," and "the woman must see to it that she pays her husband all respect" (Eph. 5:25, 22–23 NEB). What if the husband doesn't do what he's supposed to? What if the wife doesn't? Face up to it—in this world nobody gets what he is reasonably entitled to. There is the world's "solution" to this problem: fight. There is the Christian's: relinquish. God did not get what he had a right to expect—the love and obedience of the creature he had made. Instead, he got rebellion and disobedience. Adam and Eve made a general mess of everything, and we carry on making new messes daily.

We have a Script. "Let your bearing towards one another arise out of your life in Christ Jesus. For the divine nature was his from the first, yet he did not think to snatch at equality with God but made himself nothing, assuming the nature of a slave" (Phil. 2:5–6 NEB). What Christ gave up was not his divine nature (people are always worried about losing their "personhood"), but the glory that nature entitled him to. He was God by nature, and he voluntarily became a slave so that the Father would give back to him in boundless measure the glory he had given up.

What a Script! What a lesson! Christianity insists always on *the rights of others*. A Christian lays down his own life to obtain them. If he asks, Have *I* no rights? the answer is "The servant is not greater than his Lord."

Selah, Sally. Ponder that, Dick. And God help me (Elisabeth) when the next test comes. It probably won't be more than five minutes from now.

17

Is Divorce the Only Way?

Every choice in life is made in some context. Not long ago I wrote a letter to a man named Dick who chose divorce. Then I wrote about Sally, the woman he turned loose, and about some of the choices she, the "victim" or the "innocent party" must make. Now I write to both of them—with trepidation, of course, aware that probably the last thing they want to hear about from me or anybody else is reconciliation. Hopelessness has perhaps set in by now, if not pure hatred, and they are convinced that everything has been tried and found wanting. The die is cast. The divorce is long since finished, and now they have to get on with their separate lives.

The business of living a life for God is never finished, however, until we reach the gates of the City. ("Finished," did I say? But it is only then really begun!) I write to the man or woman in whose heart, even if that heart is broken or full of remorse and sin, still lies the longing to please God.

How can we do this? Well, let's not listen to any ungodly counsel. The man is called "blessed," which means happy, who walketh not in that kind of counsel (see Ps. 1:1). The trouble with the ungodly is that they have no reference point but themselves, so they try everything that looks as though it might lead to a "solution." They leave out the one thing that really matters, the thing that, although not necessarily the direct route to solutions, is the only route to happiness. "Happy is the man who does not take the wicked for his guide, nor walk the road that sinners tread. . . . The law of the Lord is his delight" (Ps. 1:1–2 NEB). That's what matters—the law of the Lord.

Not all who practice under the label "Christian" counselor are in the biblical sense godly. There is sometimes uncertainty as to the authority and relevance of "the law of the Lord," that is, of what the Bible says about human situations. "This is the end of the twentieth century," we are reminded. "There are no simple answers." I believe there are indeed some *simple* ones, but they are not *easy*. By that I mean that I can understand them—I cannot easily obey them. The road spoken of in that first psalm, the one sinners tread, is a wide one, smoothed by millions of feet. The road we must tread is narrow and rough, but we are not alone—the Holy Spirit has been "called alongside" to comfort, help, and teach us—and millions have walked the road of obedience before us.

If there is still a desire in the heart of either husband or wife for help, if there remains even the tiniest shred of forlorn hope that reconciliation is possible, might we ask first of all a question that precedes all other questions when godly counsel is sought. It is this: What is the context of our lives? There are two choices. We live our lives in the context of the world, which makes up its own rules as it goes along, or in the context of the Kingdom of God, in which the law is the Lord's.

What was the context of our conflict? Here we may run into difficulty. One or both partners may believe they did the will of God and that was what caused the conflict. Leave this one, then, and try the next: What did each of us do when the conflict arose? Was it dictated by concern for the Kingdom of God, or something else (personal happiness, perhaps)?

What is needed now to move into that heavenly Kingdom? If both partners, humbly and honestly, answer that they want to live their lives in the context of the Kingdom, and are, humbly and honestly, prepared to pay the price exacted of those who live there, I believe with all my heart that there will be a "solution."

But suppose only one of them seeks God's will in the matter. It may be the one generally called the "innocent" party. He or she is being divorced by the other. Then again, the one claiming to seek God's will may be the one who filed the papers. He or she may have sought Christian counsel, prayed, tried to patch things up, and at last, in despair, turned to the law—that is, to divorce—as the only possible thing to do. *He* thinks of himself as the innocent one. There is yet another possibility—that the one who is seeking God's will is the one most acutely aware that he *is* at fault, that he is the *guilty* party.

What I have to say to this person, whichever he is, is not offered as a solution. God does not promise solutions to all our problems. The gospel is not a guarantee of the healing of all diseases, the dissolving of all debts, the mending of all marriages, and the fulfilling of all desires *on this side of the Jordan*. The Gospel, as the good news of freedom from sin and self, is in fact also a guarantee of what Jesus called *tribulation*. You can't live as a Christian in a sinful world without tribulation. Jesus came to bring not peace but a sword. He described himself as a stone, rejected by the builders. "Any man who falls on that stone will be dashed to pieces; and if it falls on a man he will be crushed by it" (Luke 20:18 NEB). Too often we forget those stern words, or the prophecy of old Simeon when Jesus was a baby: "Many in Israel will stand or fall because of Him" (Luke 2:35 NEB).

What I have to say is infinitely more important than solutions. It is a matter of obedience. In other words, if you are the one deeply longing for help, there are answers—answers that will please God and enable you to do his will. Will they "work"? you ask. The answer is yes—in terms of the Kingdom.

But be careful. The disciple cannot test the answer in terms of earthly success or satisfaction or solutions.

Obedience might in fact lead to reconciliation and thus to the miraculous repair of what seemed a hopeless mess. But then it might not lead to any such thing. Remember what Jesus promised to those who wanted to follow? "I have come to set fire to the earth. . . . Do you suppose that I came to establish peace on earth? No indeed, I have come to bring division" (Luke 12:49, 51–52 NEB). "All will hate you for your allegiance to me. But not a hair of your head shall be lost" (Luke 21:17–18 NEB).

What did he mean? He meant that sometimes there must be the choice between obedience and a solution—between his will and, for example, self-preservation. They are not always the same thing. As a matter of fact, in the Kingdom they often turn out to be quite opposite. "Whoever cares for his own safety is lost; but if a man will let himself be lost for my sake, that man is safe" (Luke 9:24 NEB). It's either/or. It's self-death and eternal life, or it's self-life and eternal death.

Divorce often seems the way not merely to happiness, but to simple survival and sanity. Not to divorce seems suicide. "This woman is ruining my entire career." "She's not a wife/he's not a husband." "This person is destroying my personhood." "Nobody can live with a woman like her."

It is clear that no direct action on your part will change another person. You can pray that God will change him, and you can let God change you (you may be the one who needs it more!).

"No," you say, "it's hopeless. Divorce is the only way. Not to divorce would be suicide." What a dilemma! A thing God hates on one hand, suicide on the other.

I must walk very softly here. I have never been in this fix. I cannot say, "Our marriage was on the rocks and God worked a miracle for us." All I can say with confidence is that I have been in some other "fixes" in which obedience to God has appeared to be (humanly speaking) a terrible risk. At least once in my life it looked like "letting myself be lost." Suicide was not a word I used, because I was thinking in terms of Jesus's words quoted above, but it certainly was the word some people used regarding my decision.

Remember the martyr Stephen. It was witness that mattered, not self-preservation. Remember Shadrach, Meshach, and Abednego. It was witness that mattered, not self-preservation. I am not referring here to the popular use of the word *witness*— talking to somebody about his soul's salvation. I am speaking of a life laid down in obedience, whatever that obedience may entail. Such a life witnesses to love for God. One who loves him does what he says, cost what it may. Not a hair lost? No, not in terms of the Kingdom. But yes, in this world's terms, more than hair—the life itself—may be lost.

What, then, are the choices? I ask you gently and in the name of Christ, what do you really *want*? Is it Christ or happiness? Is it the will of the Father, or is it freedom from pain? Is it the Kingdom of Heaven or the kingdom of self?

If it is the Kingdom of Heaven you really want, then you can do only what fits the terms of that Kingdom. You will not be asking, "Will this solve my problem?" or "What will I gain by this?" or "What are my rights?" You will be on your knees instead, saying, "Thy kingdom come," which means "My kingdom go." You will be saying, "Thy will be done," which means "My will be undone."

"So you're saying it's absolutely wrong for anybody to divorce anybody for any reason?" No. "Well, then, what are you saying? What am I supposed to do?"

So far I have been trying to encourage you to think as a Christian. We are all deeply infected by worldly patterns of thinking and need constantly to bring our thoughts under Christ's authority. Pray for guidance. Clear up all that can be cleared up in your own heart and conscience, remembering always to act in the context of the Kingdom. The following chart may help to clarify your choices.

Which Context?

The Kingdom of Heaven	The Kingdom of Self
Thy will be done (which means my will be undone)	My will be done (which means Thy will be undone)
Losing myself and saving what matters far more	Saving myself and losing what matters far more

My aims:

another's happiness and fulfillment;	my own happiness and fulfillment;
giving;	getting;
glorifying God	satisfying myself

My object:

eternal gain	temporal gain

My right:

that of John 10:18 to lay down my life	to live life my way

My concern:

obedience	solutions

The price:

tribulation now, peace later; death to self; life forever	tribulation later, peace now; self-preservation; death forever

Christians are members of the body of Christ. As such they do not act alone or in isolation, but always with reference to other members. For a clear, biblical treatment of the many complexities of the questions that are beyond the scope of this article, see Jay E. Adams: *Marriage, Divorce, and Remarriage* (Presbyterian and Reformed Publishing Co., Phillipsburg, N.J.). Dr. Adams shows strongly the importance of the church's action in these matters. Discipline is the church's responsibility. Don't try to sort it all out alone. Go to the elders and deacons of a church where the Bible is believed to be authoritative, and submit yourself to their ruling.

It is very likely that the first task assigned you will be repentance. Whether you are the one suing for divorce or the one sued, you will have sinned *in some way, at some time,* against your spouse and against God (I do not speak from experience here). Confess every sin you can think of—every nasty thought, every sinful word or deed, everything left undone that should have been done, every attitude of rebellion and resentment and bitterness and hate. Confess them to God. Perhaps you will next have to confess to your spouse if he or she is still around and willing to listen. Remember the question asked early in this discussion—what is needed now to move into that heavenly Kingdom? This is it: repentance. Turning around 180 degrees and moving in the opposite direction. Taking a new route. Relinquishing the old.

After you have done that, you must forgive. You must forgive the other one even if he/she does not forgive you and cares not at all to be forgiven. I do not say you must give him/her a list of offenses which you are now going to cross off. Read the list only to God and cross them off in his presence. The items your spouse knows about, which you have accused him of, you will probably need to forgive him for, specifically, to his face. No matter what he or she has done (and "sides" don't matter here—there is sin on both), you must forgive.

> Since unforgiveness roots itself down in hate, Satan has room for both feet in such a heart, with all the leeway action of such purchase. That word unforgiving! What a group of relatives it has, near and far! Jealousy, envy, bitterness, the cutting word, the polished shaft of sarcasm with the poisoned tip, the green eye, the acid saliva—what kinsfolk these!
>
> S. D. Gordon, *Quiet Talks on Prayer*
> Revell, p. 79

I have known what it is to lose a husband through death but not through divorce. When my first husband died, a newly divorced friend wrote, "Don't forget there are *much* worse ways to lose one!" I have no doubt about that. I am sure a much sorer wound results from rejection or unfaithfulness than from death. The healing of such a wound must be very deep, and, as with the healing of a physical wound, there may need to be both cutting and cleansing before there can be healing. The Word cuts. Taking heed to the Word cleanses. Then God (and only God) does the healing. He creates new life and new flesh. His forgiveness for us is as boundless and just as certain as it was for his disobedient people Israel, of whom he said, "I will bring them back to this place and let them dwell there undisturbed. They shall become my people and I will become their God" (Jer. 32:37–38 NEB). It may be that the rest of that promise will be quite literally fulfilled as well: "I will give them one heart and one way of life so that they shall fear me at all times, for their own good and the good of their children after them" (v. 39).

Does it seem impossible? Then perhaps you're still thinking in the context of this world. Try the other context, the one in which all things become new and even the dead are raised.

18

Images of Hell

Somehow or other North Dakota did not seem quite the place where my husband and I expected to find the sort of television program that shocked us. We were in a motel—not one of those that offers Home Box Office or other special shows for a fee, but a perfectly ordinary one. The program that stopped us in our tracks was, we discovered, a perfectly ordinary one that is shown all over the country, twenty-four hours a day. It hasn't gotten to the Boston area as far as I know, but it will. It is rock music—the screaming, thundering, pulsating, shrieking, ear-drubbing, earsplitting, ear-bludgeoning kind, played by groups with names like Cheap Trick, the Boomtown Rats, the Sex Pistols, Missing Persons, the Destroyers, and The Clash. Across the bottom of the screen ran a legend from time to time, giving the name of the soloist, the title of the "music," and the group performing. Song titles were such things as "Screaming for Vengeance," "Bad Boy Having a Party," "Children of the Grave," "Escalator of

Life" ("I'm shoppin' the human mall" was a line from that one), "Combat Rock," "Maneater," and "Paranoid."

Songs, they're called. I had some idea that singing was supposed to touch the heart. What is the condition of the heart that is touched by titles like those? What was happening on the screen was at least as depressing. The music was being dramatized by children. They were heavily made up, of course, doing their level best to act as sophisticated, blasé, and bored as adults must seem to them, but it was plain that most of them were teenagers, early teenagers. They were slinking around bars, slouching along brilliantly lighted city streets; toying with elegant wineglasses in high-toned restaurants, smoking with long, slim, shiny cigarette holders. They were gazing dully at the camera, looking up through lowered eyebrows or down through false eyelashes. They were writhing in horizontal positions, or girls were sashaying away from boys, casting over a raised shoulder the cruel come-on glance of the vamp. Boys were striding with thrust-forward pelvises toward the girls, breathing heavily through parted lips, hulking, swaying, scowling.

The camera went from these scenes to the rock groups sweating and screaming under the colored lights, dressed in rags, blue jeans, tights, sequins, undershirts, and in some cases nearly nothing. Hair was stringy, spinachy, wild—or "punk rock," dyed, partially shaved, stiff. They smashed, hammered, clobbered those drums. They doubled up in agony over their guitars, striving, twisting, stamping, and jumping. Their faces were contorted with hatred or pain, at times jeering, insolent, defiant. Back the camera would go then to the slithering kids trying to "express themselves" or to play out the lyrics that were being yelled at top decibel by whoever was clutching the microphone. (How do their vocal cords stand it?)

But oh, the faces of those kids. I was riveted to the screen, aghast, horrified. There was a terrible fascination in the very absence of reality. How had they been programmed to erase from their fresh young faces every trace of personality, every least hint of humanity? They stared with unblinking blankness, lifeless, spiritless, cold. A strange and surreal alternative to the spastic seizures, paroxysms, and nauseated retchings of the "musicians."

This, then, is what rock music is all about. Images of hell. That's all I could think of. Hell is the place where those whose motto is *My will be done* will finally and forever get what they want. Hell is agony and blankness and torture and the absence of all that humanity was originally destined to be. The glory has terminally departed. It is the heat of flames (not of passion—that will long since have burned out) and the appalling lifelessness of solid ice, an everlasting burning and an irreversible freezing.

Tyndale House's little paper *The Church Around the World* cited a study by Columbia University that helps to explain why we get what we get on TV:

- 50 percent of those controlling the media have "no religion"
- 8 percent attend church or synagogue weekly
- 86 percent attend seldom or never
- 84 percent believe government should have no laws regulating sex
- 55 percent believe extramarital affairs are not immoral
- 95 percent believe homosexuality is not wrong
- 85 percent believe homosexuals should be permitted to teach in public schools

I do not plan a campaign to squelch rock music. It is simply an accurate expression of the powers that are at work in our society:

For the words that the mouth utters come from the overflowing of the heart. A good man produces good from the store of good within himself; and an evil man from evil within produces evil. . . . Out of your own mouth you will be acquitted; out of your own mouth you will be condemned.

Matthew 12:35–36 NEB

From racket, din, cacophony, and pandemonium ("all demons"), good Lord, deliver us. Give us the strength that comes from quietness; your gentleness, Lord, your peace. And one more thing, Lord—put a new song in our mouths, even praise to our God.

When I Was Being Made in Secret

As I drove into the yard, a boy of nine raced across the lawn with his new golden retriever puppy on a training lead.

"Aunt Betty! This is Bucky! We just got him!" Within the next few minutes, I heard all about Bucky and about Charles's new collections of stamps, baseball cards, and toy cars (among them a police car, a space vehicle, a green hatchback, a Volkswagen with oversize tires, and a model of "Le Car"), as well as about his golf lessons ("I got a set of clubs, too!"), tennis lessons ("Look at my new racquet!"), the Christmas cards he was selling in order to win prizes, and about sleeping on the screened porch in a sleeping bag.

Nothing extraordinary or astonishing about this nine-year-old. He's lively, he has a very wide grin, he wears ragged cutoffs, and he even chopped up his shirt with scissors (collar and sleeves were too hot, he explained). His blond hair sticks out in funny places, and his striped tennis shoes seem as clumsily huge as Mickey Mouse's always did.

But yesterday when I visited this charming nephew of mine, I thought of some people I saw last month when I went to a hospital in Mississippi to visit my new granddaughter Elisabeth. I peered eagerly through the nursery window along with all the other grandmothers and the smug fathers. "Ours" was shown to us by the nurse, a beautiful tiny thing clenching her perfect fists. I gazed as enthralled as though I had never seen a newborn child, as though Elisabeth were the first of her kind ever to appear to mystify and bewitch and melt the soul of a grandmother.

It was at the back of the nursery that I saw the people who affected me very differently but also very deeply. They were extremely small. A nurse thrust her hands into built-in rubber gloves in the side of an incubator and ever so gently lifted a little creature that looked infinitely more fragile and helpless than our baby, a "preemie" of perhaps two and a half pounds. He was one of several in incubators, and as I watched them lying there, eyes bandaged against the heat lamp, moving and breathing in their plastic boxes, I thought of Charles, who was just such a baby nine years ago. Born three months early, he was not expected to make it through the first night.

Earnestly prayed for by his parents and many others, cared for continuously by many hands as gentle as those of the nurse I watched in Mississippi, he survived.

Not long ago I saw a picture that will remain ineradicable in my mind: a black plastic garbage bag which contained what was left of the morning's work in one city hospital—four or five babies, some of them the size of Charles when he was born, some of them larger. They were rejects.

Who is it that makes the "selections"? Who may determine which tiny person is acceptable and may be permitted to be born (and if necessary, hovered over, cradled in a sterile temperature-controlled incubator to assist his survival), and which is unacceptable and may be treated as a cancer or a gangrenous growth and surgically or chemically removed? What perverted vision of "life enhancement" warrants such a choice?

Gloria Steinem appeared on television recently to speak about what she calls "pro-choice." What she did not say, what no proponent of abortion ever says, is that the choice they defend is the choice to kill people. Babies are people, but the U.S. Supreme Court has decreed that certain people, if they are young enough and helpless enough, may be killed.

Another choice the courts and modern liberality and morality permit us to make is the choice of a tasteful vocabulary. To begin with, the rejects I saw in the plastic bag were not babies, they were not people, they were, if small enough and unrecognizable enough, merely "tissue" or, as ethicist Charles Curran puts it, "the matter involved in the research." If undeniably identifiable, they were but the "products of conception." Well, so is Charles. So am I.

Words most assiduously to be avoided are "kill" and "murder." They were also avoided by the physicians who supervised the "selections" in Nazi concentration camps. Heirs to Europe's proudest medical traditions, they resorted to complicated mental gymnastics to provide moral and scientific legitimacy for Hitler's crazed racial and biological notions. In a world forty years advanced from those barbarities, we speak of freedom, of the liberation of women, of the right over our own bodies—viewing ourselves as emancipated and enlightened while we sink into ever more diabolical (though always finely calculated and carefully rationalized) modes of self-worship and idolatry.

When anyone has the indelicacy to call a spade a spade (i.e., an abortion a murder), he is accused (as in *Time*, July 30, 1979) of "hateful propaganda, harassment, disregard of other people's civil rights . . . an attempt to force [his] own perception of morality on everyone else." It was Uta Landy, executive director of the National Abortion Federation in New York, who wrote that.

Shall we, like those idealists in Germany, in order to evade the real horror, invoke such forms of self-delusion and insist on innocuous and deceptive terms like "procedure" or "loss"

111

instead of "killing," or "tissue" for "child"? While we pharisaically deplore Malaysia's management of the pitiful "boat people" (the Home Affairs Minister, Ghazali bin Shafie, said, "The Vietnamese keep throwing rubbish into our gardens"), we rationalize and legalize—we even feel it our duty to facilitate and finance—the disposal of tens of thousands of—what shall we call them if not *people*?

I could not miss the ironies of *The New Yorker's* editorializing about Malaysia. Not many months ago it threw up its hands in horror at those who would oppose "the right to choose" abortion. Now it points out that it is the policy of our government to favor human rights around the world, yet "one of the earth's peoples is being set adrift on the high seas, and in the whole wide world there is no dependable place of refuge."

Let us who claim to accept moral responsibility for refugees and the world's rejects remember that another of earth's peoples is being "selected," shall we say, for annihilation. We are accused of insensitivity if we mention the black plastic garbage bags or saline burning or the intrauterine dismemberment of gestating human beings, but in the whole wide world is there for them "no dependable place of refuge"?

Let us consider these things in quietness before God who sees them all. "O Lord, thou hast searched me and known me ... my frame was not hidden from thee, when I was being made in secret. . . . Thy eyes beheld my unformed substance; in thy book were written, every one of them, the days that were formed for me, when as yet there was none of them. . . . See if there be any wicked way in me, and lead me in the way everlasting" (Ps. 139:1, 15, 16, 24 RSV).

20

London Diary

Maundy Thursday TWA out of Boston at 8:30 p.m. Huge plane, a 1011, every seat full—at least a third of them, it seems, with kids on vacation. (If they go to England for spring vacation when they're in the ninth grade, what do they do in the tenth?)

I am in row 27 next to a woman who is traveling with the two women in front of us. Steward pauses in aisle: "Excuse me, ladies, are you traveling together?" he asks me. "No." He studies the paper in his hand. "Well, you see, I need these seats." My hopes soar. Once before in my life I've heard this and been moved up to first class. "I'll be happy to change," I tell him. My seatmate explains that she is traveling with the others. "Must you travel together?" he asks, still studying his seating chart. "Yes." Long pause. "Well, then, I'll take the three of you." Off they go to first class, elated. I, deflated, stay in tourist class.

Dinner served at 11:00 p.m. I doze off when the movie begins. Shortly after midnight, Eastern Standard Time, sky turns orange. At 1:00 they bring breakfast and at 2:00 we are at Heathrow Airport.

Good Friday I breeze through passage marked "Nothing to Declare." Mary, former missionary colleague from Ecuador, bursts from crowd, runs toward me grinning. Friend with car (which we cannot find for some time—he forgets which level he parked it on) drives us to Mary's flat, stopping in Kew Gardens. "Come down to Kew in lilac time . . . it isn't far from London." But it is too early for lilacs. Tulips and daffodils in abundance. Lovely freshness, greenness of new spring grass, budding trees. Bicycles, baby carriages, strollers. People on benches, being blessed by sun. Hideous scream of 747s overhead, directly on landing pattern for Heathrow. (It is nice to be a privileged person inside one. Now I am an annoyed person under one.)

Mary's flat in East Dulwich (pronounced Dullage) very tiny. In row of houses called "terraces," of which England has millions. Every house has two stories, two chimneys, four chimney pots. Bay window on each floor, brightly painted trim (liver green, electric blue, lavender are favorites), four-foot square "garden" in front with hedge and/or wall and gate. Tiny cars parked in street. Flat has living room "lounge," single bedroom, bath, and diminutive kitchen. Tiny stove, tiny refrigerator, tiny sink. To an English housewife, surely, everything in my kitchen would be huge—unnecessarily, perhaps outrageously, huge. In lounge are seven chairs, three small tables, bookcases, two electric heaters, two afghans, two candlesticks, two Ecuadorian paintings, two wood carvings, thirteen Easter cards taped to back of door.

Jet lag. Afternoon nap. Mary gives me bedroom, sleeps on floor of lounge. Bach's *St. Matthew Passion*, sung from Lincoln Cathedral, is on the "telly" when I awake. Followed by Stainer's *Crucifixion*.

Saturday Red double-decker bus to Tottenham Court Road. Lecture on Elgin (the *g* is hard) Marbles at British Museum. We see the Marbles—the frieze removed from the

Parthenon by Lord Elgin in order to preserve it. Sublime, almost alive. 192 men on horseback. Men mounted on horses in Greek sculpture represent heroes. Herodotus, the lecturer tells us, reported 192 men killed in the Battle of Marathon. Rosetta Stone. Mummy from 3000 B.C., body in fetal position, hair still intact. Library closed. E. M. Forster's childhood letters on display.

Easter Vigil at All Saints, Margaret Street. Total darkness, fire kindled in courtyard, candles in hands of all worshippers, music, litany, then darkness again. Sudden burst of light and organ music, the ringing of many bells. *He is risen!*

Easter Sunday Westminster Abbey, founded by Edward the Confessor in 1065, originally a Benedictine monastery with an enclosed choir in which the monks sang offices. We sit in choir, close to boy singers, their music and discipline nearly perfect. Hymn from Medieval Latin with seventeenth-century German melody: "Light's glittering morn bedecks the sky; Heaven thunders forth its victor-cry: Alleluia!" A black man opposite me sings every word from memory, his face radiant.

The prayers: "To Thee we give high praise and hearty thanks . . . above all for Thine inestimable love in giving Thine only Son, our Saviour Jesus Christ . . . He made a full, perfect, and sufficient sacrifice for the sins of the whole world. . . ." For nine hundred years of sinners who met in this one place—kings, queens, monks, tailors, candlestick makers, tourists. Prayers and hymns ascend from all of them through these arches and clerestories, unknown to one another, fully known to God, fully loved. Wesley's hymn, "Vain the stone, the watch, the seal, Christ hath burst the gates of hell!" Sermon by the dean of the abbey: "The splendor of Easter is born out of the dereliction of the Cross."

Tombs, sarcophagi, memorial tablets—"In memory of the people who served in the Sudan," "In memory of twenty-six monks who died in the Black Death, 1342." David Livingstone, "brought by faithful hands over land and sea." Tablets commemorating a plumber and a musician who served the abbey. Bells ring from the steeples, Big Ben chimes as we leave.

Victoria Embankment Gardens. Daffodils, daffodils, daffodils. Blackbirds singing. Sunshine. Statue of William Tyndale, 1484–1536. He prayed before his martyrdom, "Lord, open the King of England's eyes." A year later, says the inscription, a Bible was placed in every church by the king's command. All London—all Europe and India, in fact—seem to be on the embankment. Sunday papers, queues for the tour boats, iced lollies, cameras. At St. Paul's a notice: "Please do not carry ice creams into the cathedral." We obey.

Monday To Waltham Abbey, founded by King Harold in 1066. Waltham Cross, erected at one of the stations where King Edward halted in his journey to bring the body of his queen Eleanor from the north to London. Tea with Mary's friend, Gae, in her old country house. Hot cross buns, cake. Gae's nephew, Mark, three years old, in cultured English accent, asks, "May I show you the lawn mowah?" To the garden shed. "This one is the fly (i.e., rotary) mowah. It spreads the grass all over the place! And this one is the blade mowah." Someone tells Mark that I have a grandson, Walter. "Has his daddy got a fly mowah?" he asks at once.

Tuesday I speak at Peckham Road Gospel Hall. Tea and cakes beforehand. ("Gracious living does take time," my sister-in-law once remarked.) Old ladies in brimless, cushionlike hats, winter coats. One of them sees a picture of my daughter Valerie: "She looks an absolute poppet!" Many West Indians in audience. A lady whispers to me afterwards, "You are the first woman my husband has ever listened to!"

Wednesday I speak at St. Patrick's Church, Wallington. The canon takes me home for dinner. Ham, creamed (i.e., mashed) potatoes, roast potatoes, peas, beans, trifle. Lady at table says, "But of course Americans have many domestic servants!" In my talk at the church I mention Edith Cherry's hymn, "We Rest on Thee, Our Shield and Our Defender," speaking of how five missionaries in Ecuador sang it and then were speared to death. Our faith must embrace this, as did the faith of John the Baptist who lost his head and of Stephen who was stoned to death. Man says to me later, "That hymn will never be the same to me again." People who want autographs queue very politely. Another difference from Americans.

Thursday Taxi, bus, train to Edenbridge. Taxi driver, asked how he'd like a woman prime minister, says, "Ah've got one woman over me now—and a good one, mind, Ah'm not complainin'—but I don't want another one!" Bus driver: "That's right, ducks, up you go!" Trainman: "Come along, love!" Station buffet offers pork pie, steak-and-kidney pie, sausage rolls, chocolate biscuits, coffee, tea, bovril, mineral water. No hot dogs, milk shakes, Fritos. From the train we see small houses, small gardens, small cars, small people, small shops. English economy. No wonder. It's a small island. No wonder Americans seem crass and extravagant. In one garden we see espaliered fruit trees (trained to grow flat on a trellis), a wonderful economy of space.

Friday Coach from Marylebone Station to Derbyshire, where I am to speak at a conference of the South American Missionary Society. (I learn that a bus is red, and double-decker. A coach is what Americans would call a bus, usually chartered.) Women clutching umbrellas, shopping bags (*all* English women, I think, have shopping bags), thermos "flasks," sandwiches, chattering happily. Men with briefcases, sweaters underneath suitcoats, earnestly discuss mission strategy. An Australian woman across the aisle is the only one wearing makeup. English countryside—hedgerows, green pastures, daffodils (they seem to grow wild), rooks' nests in bare trees. Man flies a red kite that has a blue tail. Clean new lambs with black faces and black legs caper around placid weather-stained ewes. "Little lamb, God bless thee!"

Lorries, which outnumber cars on the motorway, are labeled "Bird's Custard," "Removals and Haulage," "Walker's Potato Crisps," "King's Road Tyres."

Swanwick (pronounced Swanick), a once lovely country house turned into a conference center. Wallpaper in my room: yellow, green, orange flowers, each eighteen inches in diameter. Carpet: red and black. Bedspread: brown. Curtains: purple and brown. Hallway: green and purple striped wallpaper, red and blue striped carpet, turquoise woodwork, lavender doors. Outdoors, loveliness everywhere. Formal gardens, pastures with cows, pond, rolling meadows, blackbirds. Daffodils, of course.

Saturday Meetings in morning. A Latin American evangelist, a bishop from Chile, an ex-missionary from Ecuador. Afternoon: drive to Matlock where we have a "cream tea"—tea, scones, thick "clotted" cream, strawberry jam.

Sunday Archbishop Donald Coggan preaches a brief and moving sermon from John 20: "He came . . . stood . . . spoke . . . showed . . . breathed. So He comes to us, frightened at the unknown. . . ." At lunch Major Somebody talks to me about how to minister to widows. A young man speaks of how his own life was changed—he became a missionary with SAMS—because of the testimony of Jim Elliot. I am driven to London by a Baptist minister who attended conference. Stay with a friend in elegant flat in Kensington. Fifteen-foot ceilings, beautiful mouldings, antique furniture, fabrics all designed by my friend Leonie herself.

Monday Shopping at Harrod's department store. I buy small leather books, Beatrix Potter table mats for friends. In the Food Hall hundreds of sausages, hams, cheeses suspended from lofty ceiling. Great slabs of smoked salmon. Cans of ox tongues. In the garden furniture department, real fruit on the tables, a real tree bearing limes. Could this be anywhere but in England, anywhere else than Harrod's? Lunch at Simpson's—roast beef and Yorkshire pudding. Good-bye to Mary and Gae at air terminal. Gae says Mark has informed everyone this week that Waltah's daddy has a fly mowah.

Leave London on TWA, 5:00 p.m., Daylight Time. Reach U.S. 6:30 p.m., Eastern Standard Time, after seven hours' flight.

I go over my notes. Only a travelogue. A few highlights from many things that seemed to happen in an instant of time. The distance is hard to grasp, having been swallowed up with such speed—rushing into dawn one night, rushing back toward the sunset so fast it hadn't time to fade but hovered stationary on the horizon for seven hours.

Strangely, the vignettes that stay with me were not in the diary notes. A "punch-up" on the sidewalk below Mary's window as we sat at tea. Two women screaming obscenities (some of them new to me), kicking each other in the face, pulling hair, rolling on the street. The desperation of their empty lives tore at my imagination.

The tall sorrowful woman in purple in Westminster Abbey. A purple crocheted hat with ribbons, two long gray pigtails, a flowing purple silk scarf, long purple skirt, purple shoes. She stood gazing at something high above her.

The taxi driver who refused to take us home late following the vigil. "Well, thanks anyway," Mary called. "Have a Happy Easter!"

"Oh, I could never have that, love," he said. "My wife's just got cancer."

> Lord, by the stripes which wounded Thee
> From death's dread sting Thy servants free
> That we may live and sing to Thee, Alleluia!

119

How to Sell Yourself

A couple of hundred secretaries attended a seminar in Syracuse a few months ago. Because I happened to be in the hotel that day, I did a little eavesdropping.

The speaker was a snappily dressed, fast-talking Yuppie who dished out a lot of expensive advice about how to sell yourself in the business world. By the way you dress, she explained, you can put across a message of power (suits, ladies, not soft sweaters; skirts, not slacks; pumps, not sandals).

The way you wear your hair tells the boss more than your resume did. Hair over the forehead tells him (yes, the lecturer did actually refer to the boss as "him" most of the time) you're shy, coy, or afraid of something; long, loose stuff says you haven't grown up. And you *know* what fluffed-out hair proclaims the minute you walk into the office: fluffbrain!

What you eat for lunch and how you arrange your desk lets people know who's in charge. No creamed dishes, no desserts; no teddy bears or cutesy mottoes on the desk. Feel good about yourself—slim, trim, lots of vim. Be assertive. Be confident. Walk into the head office in your elegant Joseph A. Bank suit—dark (of course) impeccably (of course) tailored (of course). Stand tall. Head up. Smile. Give him the kind of handshake that lets him know it could have been a knuckle-cruncher—he'll get the message: *power*. You're in charge.

Beneath the Surface

In *Tree of Life* magazine Peter Reinhart writes:

> The spirit of this age is one of personal power; the spirit of Christ is one of humility. The spirit of this age is one of ambitious accomplishment; the spirit of Christ is one of poverty. The spirit of this age is one of self-determination; the spirit of Christ is one of abandonment to Divine Providence.

He goes on to suggest a new kind of seminar: training in the assertion of *virtues*—humility, for example, spiritual poverty, purity of heart, chastity of mind. Instead of self-reliance, he sees reliance on Christ as the source of empowerment and liberation.

So do I. To be Christ's slave is perfect freedom.

Will this idea sell? Will it work? Can we really get what we want this way? The third question is the crucial one for Christians. Answer it, and you already have the answer to the first two.

If what you want is what the world wants, nobody will be able to sell Reinhart's seminar to you. It isn't going to work.

But if you've made up your mind to have what the world despises—the things that last forever—and if Jesus Christ is Lord of your life, the whole picture, even in the dog-eat-dog world of competition and big money and big success, will be different.

What distinguishes the Christian from others in that world? I admit the validity of some of the Yuppie's advice, silly as it sounds. The medium, also, *is* to a certain extent the message. A Christian must be at least as careful, sensible, and serious about doing the job properly as anybody else. He must also dress and act carefully, sensibly, seriously. Man looks on the outward appearance because it's the only thing man can look on. God alone can look on the heart.

What's in the heart reveals itself sooner or later. You may get the job on the basis of first appearance. You'll keep it on the basis of how you perform day by day. Many perform well because they're after money and power—but there's nearly always room for a little fudging here and there, a lot of elbowing and shoving and downright trampling of whoever's in your way, not to mention high-level crimes that people get away with.

The Christian in the office or factory or construction job operates from a wholly different motive: "service rendered to Christ himself, not with the idea of currying favor with men, but as the servants of Christ conscientiously doing what you believe to be the will of God for you" (Eph. 6:5–6 Phillips).

How High, How Mighty?

I would hope that the Christian businessman or woman, whether lowest on the corporate totem pole or the chief executive officer, would be distinguished from the rest not only by conscientious work but also by graciousness, by simple kindness, by an unassuming manliness or a modest womanliness, and above all by a readiness to serve. There's nothing intrinsically wrong with ambition—Jesus often appealed to it—but the nature of those ambitions makes a huge difference: "He that would be chief among you must be servant of all," even if that means serving coffee instead of serving on the committee you were itching to join.

A Christian is the sort of person who can be asked to do whatever needs to be done without retorting, "That's not *my* job." Somebody is bound to remind me that you can get in trouble with the unions this way. Well, you know what I mean. Christians are *available*. Christians aren't too high and mighty to do the nasty little task nobody else will do. Christians can be counted on, imposed on, sometimes walked all over. Why not? Their Master was.

I think of my friend Betty Greene, a pilot (called an aviator in her early days) who ferried bombers during World War II and helped found Mission Aviation Fellowship. "I made up my mind," she told me, "that if I was to make it in a man's world, I would have to be a lady." A more ladylike lady I have never known. She knows when to keep her mouth shut. She's modest. She's the very soul of graciousness. She isn't trying to prove anything. Nate Saint, an early colleague of hers, once told me he had had no use for women pilots until he met Betty. She shook up his categories.

Christians ought to be always shaking up people's categories. I guess one of the things the world finds most infuriating about much-maligned Jerry Falwell is his unflappable graciousness, his refusal to retreat behind spurious logic. They'd like to call him a rednecked bigot, but he doesn't fit the category. His worst offense is that he's so often right. He speaks the truth—that's bad enough—and he speaks it in love. That's unforgivable.

"The very spring of our actions," said the apostle Paul, "is the love of Christ." That goes for all of us who claim the name *Christian*. It is the energizing principle of whatever we do—from praying and serving the church to laundry and lawn mowing and the jobs we get paid for. Charity is the word.

Charity? In the late twentieth century? Yes. If in home, school, and workplace the rule of each Christian's life were MY LIFE FOR YOURS ("in honor preferring one another") it would make a very great difference.

The Christian's distinctive mark is love. It was what set the Lord Jesus apart from all others. It was, in the end, what got him crucified. If we follow him in the marketplace, many of the self-promotion methods others use will be out of the question to us.

Won't we run the risks of being ignored, stepped on at times, passed over for a promotion? Yes, those and a good many others. But what price are we willing to pay for obedience? The faithful, unconcerned about self-actualization, will find along the pathway of self-denial the blossoms of fulfillment. We have our Lord's paradoxical promise in Luke 17:33: "Whoever tries to preserve his life will lose it, and the man who is prepared to lose his life will preserve it" (Phillips).

22

Meeting God Alone

Avery tall man, wrapped in a steamer rug, kneeling alone by a chair. When I think of my father, who died in 1963, this is often the first image that comes to mind. It was the habit of his life to rise early in the morning—usually between 4:30 and 5:00 a.m.—to study his Bible and to pray.

We did not often see him during that solitary hour (he purposed to make it solitary), but we were used to seeing him on his knees. He had family prayers every morning after breakfast. We began with a hymn; then he read from the Bible to us; and we all knelt to pray. As we grew older, we were encouraged to pray alone as well.

Few people know what to do with solitude when it is forced upon them; even fewer arrange for solitude regularly. This is not to suggest that we should neglect meeting with other believers for prayer (see Heb. 10:25), but the foundation of our devotional life is our own private relationship with God.

125

My father, an honest and humble disciple of the Lord Jesus, wanted to follow his example: "Very early in the morning . . . Jesus got up, left the house and went off to a solitary place, where he prayed" (Mark 1:35 NIV).

Christians may (and ought to) pray anytime and anywhere, but we cannot well do without a special time and place to be alone with God. Most of us find that early morning is not an easy time to pray. I wonder if there is an *easy* time.

The simple fact is that early morning is probably the *only* time when we can be fairly sure of not being interrupted. Where can we go? Into "your closet," was what the Lord said in Matthew 6:6, meaning any place apart from the eyes and the ears of others. Jesus went to the hills, to the wilderness, to a garden; the apostles to the seashore or to an upper room; Peter to a housetop.

We may need to find a literal closet or a bathroom or a parked car. We may walk outdoors and pray. But we must *arrange* to pray, to be alone with God sometime every day, to talk to him and to listen to what he wants to say to us.

The Bible is God's message to everybody. We deceive ourselves if we claim to want to hear his voice but neglect the primary channel through which it comes. We must read his Word. We must obey it. We must live it, which means rereading it throughout our lives. I think my father read it more than forty times.

When we have heard God speak, what then shall we say to God? In an emergency or when we suddenly need help, the words come easily: "Oh, God!" or "Lord, help me!" During our quiet time, however, it is a good thing to remember that we are here not to pester God but to adore him.

All creation praises him all the time—the winds, the tides, the oceans, the rivers, move in obedience; the song sparrow and the wonderful burrowing wombat, the molecules in their cells, the stars in their courses, the singing whales and the burning seraphim do without protest or slovenliness exactly what their Maker intended, and thus praise him.

We read that our heavenly Father actually looks for people who will worship him in spirit and in reality. Imagine! God is *looking for* worshippers. Will he always have to go to a church to find them, or might there be one here and there in an ordinary house, kneeling alone by a chair, simply adoring him?

How do we adore him? Adoration is not merely unselfish. It doesn't even take into consideration that the self exists. It is utterly consumed with the object adored.

Once in a while, a human face registers adoration. The groom in a wedding may seem to worship the approaching bride, but usually he has a few thoughts for himself—how does he look in this absurd ruffled shirt that she asked him to wear, what should he do with his hands at this moment, what if he messes up the vows?

I have seen adoration more than once on faces in a crowd surrounding a celebrity, but only when they were unaware of the television cameras, and only when there was not the remotest possibility that the celebrity would notice them. For a few seconds, they forgot themselves altogether.

When I stumble out of bed in the morning, put on a robe, and go into my study, words do not spring spontaneously to my lips—other than words like, "Lord, here I am again to talk to you. It's cold. I'm not feeling terribly spiritual. . . ." Who can go on and on like that morning after morning, and who can bear to listen to it day after day?

I need help in order to worship God. Nothing helps me more than the Psalms. Here we find human cries—of praise, adoration, anguish, complaint, petition. There is an immediacy, an authenticity, about those cries. They speak for me to God—that is, they say what I often want to say, but for which I cannot find words.

Surely the Holy Spirit preserved those Psalms in order that we might have paradigms of prayer and of our individual dealings with God. It is immensely comforting to find that even David, the great king, wailed about his loneliness, his enemies, his pains, his sorrows, and his fears. But then he turned from them to God in paeans of praise.

He found expression for praise far beyond my poor powers, so I use his and am lifted out of myself, up into heights of adoration, even though I'm still the same ordinary woman alone in the same little room.

Another source of assistance for me has been the great hymns of the church, such as "Praise, My Soul, the King of Heaven," "New Every Morning Is the Love," "Great Is Thy Faithfulness," "Glorious Things of Thee Are Spoken," and "O Worship the King." The third stanza of that last one delights me. It must delight God when I sing it to him:

> Thy bountiful care, what tongue can recite?
> It breathes in the air, it shines in the light;
> It streams from the hills, it descends to the plain,
> And sweetly distills in the dew and the rain.

That's praise. By putting into words things on earth for which we thank him, we are training ourselves to be ever more aware of such things as we live our lives. It is easy otherwise to be oblivious to the thousand evidences of his care. Have you thought of thanking God for light and air, because in them his care breathes and shines?

Hymns often combine praise and petition, which are appropriate for that time alone with God. The beautiful morning hymn "Awake, My Soul, and With the Sun" has these stanzas:

> All praise to Thee, who safe hast kept,
> And hast refreshed me while I slept.
> Grant, Lord, when I from death shall wake,
> I may of endless light partake.
> Direct, control, suggest, this day,
> All I design, or do, or say;
> That all my powers, with all their might,
> In Thy sole glory may unite.

128

Adoration should be followed by confession. Sometimes it happens that I can think of nothing that needs confessing. This is usually a sign that I'm not paying attention. I need to read the Bible. If I read it with prayer that the Holy Spirit will open my eyes to this need, I soon remember things done that ought not to have been done and things undone that ought to have been done.

Sometimes I follow confession of sin with confession of faith—that is, with a declaration of what I believe. Any one of the creeds helps here, or these simple words: "Christ has died; Christ is risen; Christ will come again. Lord, I believe; help my unbelief."

Then comes intercession, the hardest work in the world—the giving of one's self, time, strength, energy, and attention to the needs of others in a way that no one but God sees, no one but God will do anything about, and no one but God will ever reward you for.

Do you know what to pray for people whom you haven't heard from in a long time? I don't. So I often use the prayers of the New Testament, so all-encompassing, so directed toward things of true and eternal importance, such as Paul's for the Christians in Ephesus: ". . . I pray that you, rooted and founded in love yourselves, may be able to grasp . . . how wide and long and deep and high is the love of Christ" (Eph. 3:17–18 Phillips). Or I use his prayer for the Colossians, "We pray that you will be strengthened from God's boundless resources, so that you will find yourselves able to pass through any experience and endure it with joy" (Col. 1:11 Phillips). I have included many New Testament prayers in a small booklet entitled *And When You Pray* (Good News Publishers).

My own devotional life is very far from being Exhibit A of what it should be. I have tried, throughout most of my life, to maintain a quiet time with God, with many lapses and failures. Occasionally, but only occasionally, it is impossible. Our heavenly Father knows all about those occasions. He understands perfectly why mothers with small children bring them along when they talk to him.

Nearly always it is possible for most of us, with effort and planning and the will to do his will, to set aside time for God alone. I am sure I have lost out spiritually when I have missed that time. And I can say with the psalmist, "I have found more joy along the path of thy instruction than in any kind of wealth" (Ps. 119:14 NEB).

The Song of the Animals

The seagulls who daily fly past our house have a regular pattern: east to the rock called Norman's Woe in the morning, west to Kettle Island in the evening, with the setting sun rouging their feathers to glowing pink. Sometimes, in a strong wind, they sail up and over our house, but they do not land nearer than the sea-washed rocks. One day I was surprised to find a lone gull sitting on our deck. There was something odd about the way he sat and the shape of his head. Moving to the window I saw that he had the plastic rings from a six-pack of drinks clamped in his bill and circling his neck. He sat very quietly, a little hunched, his head tipped inquiringly. He was caught in the rings, unable to close his beak. Was he perhaps, by daring to perch on our deck, asking for help? Slowly I opened the door and tiptoed toward him. His fierce bright eyes followed me unblinking, but he did not move. When, incredulous, I nearly touched him, off he flew.

Captive to one of the complicated "blessings" of civilization that seagulls were never meant to cope with, my gull will have starved to death by now.

That ninety seconds or so on our deck brought to focus once more a phrase I turn over and over in my mind: the redemption of creation.

"Redemption? But animals have no *souls!*" someone objects. Have they not? My Bible tells me of a great hope shared not only by angels and men and women, but "all things, whether in heaven or on earth" (Col. 1:20 NEB); it tells me that *all* is to be "brought into a unity in Christ" (Eph. 1:10 NEB). What can this mean if not that in some way unimaginable to us now the suffering seagull, along with all feathered, furred, scaled, and carapaced creatures, will be redeemed? "The created universe waits with eager expectation for God's sons to be revealed" (Rom. 8:19 NEB). Will not our ears someday hear the Song of the Animals? I think so. I pin my hopes on the vision of John: "Then I heard every created thing in heaven and on earth and under the earth and in the sea, all that is in them, crying, 'Praise and honor, glory and might, to him who sits on the throne and to the Lamb for ever and ever!'" (Rev. 5:13 NEB).

24

We've Come a Long Way— or Have We?

Nowadays Christian women seem to be operating on the premise that they're perfectly free to do anything they like, including work outside the home. Whether they're young, middle-aged, or old, married or single, with children or without, droves of Christian women are now career-minded.

Isn't that okay? I'm not sure it is. Francis Schaeffer, shortly before he died, said, "Tell me what the world is saying now, and I'll tell you what the Church will be saying seven years from now." Careerism is one of the great cries of the feminist movement, and Christian women seem to be trotting along quite willingly, though perhaps five or seven years behind the secularists, tickled pink that "we've come a long way, baby."

Well, we certainly have. But is it in the right direction? Have Christian women's seminars, Christian books (and, dare I suggest it, Christian women's magazines), encouraged us, by the tacit acceptance of notions not carefully examined, to move in a direction that does not lead to freedom at all?

It's interesting to note a growing swell of disillusionment among women of the world. They're beginning to discover that the "fulfillment" they had sought in the business or professional world hasn't proved to be all that fulfilling. For many of them it's more like a sucked-out lemon.

Not long ago on *The Today Show* Jane Pauley hosted a TV special on working women. She's one herself, and I have a hunch she was wondering if other women had any unconfessed misgivings about the joys of a career. Is a career really stimulating? Is it really more "creative" than mothering or homemaking? Is it satisfying? Is it fun? Has it brought the fulfillment it promised? Her show was not a parade of happy faces. Women actually looked straight into the cameras and admitted they'd been had. They were willing to change their whole lifestyle, make sacrifices, do whatever was necessary, to get out of the work world. Several hard-driving executive types said they were going home to take care of their children. One newspaper columnist described the results of the new forms of child rearing as "emotional carnage."

Two psychologists, one from Yale, one from Harvard, have echoed these career women's misgivings, stating that what we are doing to our children now may be the equivalent of "psychological thalidomide." It's sobering to me to think that we may be maiming our children by depriving them of normal home life.

"You've got to be kidding," I hear someone say. "You aren't going to tell me that women with children aren't supposed to be working?" I'd be crazy to try to tell anybody that unless I had some authority more convincing than my personal bias. I think I have. It's a clear and simple list of things godly women—all of them—are meant to do, and it's found in Paul's instructions to a young pastor (Titus 2:3–5):

> Likewise, teach the older women to be reverent in the way they live, not to be slanderers or addicted to much wine, but to teach what is good. Then they can train the younger women to love their husbands and children, to be self-controlled and pure, to be busy at home, to be kind, and to be subject to their husbands, so that no one will malign the word of God (NEB).

Might there be a pattern in these verses that we've ignored? I've met women lately who had jumped on the careerism bandwagon but have now discovered the Bible's pattern (more of it can be found in 1 Tim. 5). Realizing that the lifestyle they've been pursuing doesn't fit the biblical pattern, they are making drastic changes. For some of them the cost has been high, but not too high for the liberation that comes with honest obedience.

I'm one of those older women Paul refers to. If I'm a Christian, I am bound by what Scripture tells me to do (there's no Christianity without obedience). By every means open to me, I am to "teach," that is, to set an example, to be a model for younger women—by reverence; by self-control; by being a loving wife and mother; pure; kind; working *at home*; respecting the authority of my husband; prayerful; worshipful; hospitable; willing to do humble and dirty jobs; taking "every opportunity of doing good" (1 Tim. 5:10 NEB).

That's a tall order. Who of us is sufficient for these things? None of us, of course, without a large portion of the grace of God every minute of every day. But if we will trust him for that grace, we must be sure our wills are lined up with his and our lives ordered according to his pattern.

There are many "buts" in our minds whenever we face truthfully any of God's clear directive. I am well aware of the thousands of women without men who must find some way to support themselves and their children. The Lord who gave us his pattern also knows intimately every situation: "Your heavenly Father knows that you need these things." Might he have another way than the one which seems inevitable? Might there be a way to work at home? How serious are we about following him? Whoever is willing to obey will be shown the way.

25

The Christian's Safety

One afternoon more than twenty years ago I was sitting in a hammock in eastern Ecuador. On the floor of my thatched house sat Minkayi, an Auca Indian, telling a story into the plastic microphone of a battery-powered tape recorder:

"One morning I had gone a short distance in my canoe when I heard the knocking of another man's canoe pole. It was Dabu. 'Are you going home?' I asked him. 'Yes,' he said. 'Naenkiwi says those foreigners are cannibals.' Later I found Gikita in his house. He said he was going to get some spears. My spears were not far away.

"Soon I found Gikita and Dyuwi putting red dye on their spears, getting them ready. 'Naenkiwi says those foreigners are going to eat us,' they told me. I still had not dyed my spears, but when afternoon came they had all dyed theirs and I was just sitting there. Finally I told my mother to go down and bring my spears up so I could dye them. 'Just bring a few,' I

137

said, and off she went. I asked Naenkiwi how many spears he had. 'Two hard ones and two lightweight ones,' he said."

Rummaging in the old footlocker in the basement years later I found my transcript of Minkayi's story. Six pages long, it was a minutely detailed account of how six Indian men ambushed five Americans one hot Sunday afternoon on a sandspit of the Curaray River.

Minkayi got quite excited telling the story. He described the journey to the beach, up hills, across rivers, through an old clearing where he had once seen a jaguar, finally reaching the place where they knew a small plane had landed. He told how one foreigner was walking up and down the beach, calling and calling. "Come!" he was saying. "Come in a friendly way, come without harm!"

Then, with vivid sound effects which I had transcribed phonetically, Minkayi told of the sudden rush with spears, accompanied by Auca war cries, and of the sounds the spears made hitting their targets. He did not spare the details of the long struggle, the suffering, and the Indians' final victory.

As I read the words, memory brought into sharp focus the cheerful, friendly man holding the microphone. Minkayi knew, of course, that one of the supposed cannibals had been my husband. When he had finished his tale, he picked up Jim's picture from the top of the kerosene boxes that served as my bookcase.

"Look at him smiling at us!" he said. "If we had known him as we know you, he'd be sitting here smiling with us this morning. A cannibal! We thought he was a cannibal!" I remembered how his face broke into a grin.

God is God. That was the stunning lesson of that most stunning event in my life. Jim's death required me to deny God or believe him, to trust him or renounce him. The lesson is the same for all of us. The contexts differ.

There was nothing new to Minkayi about killing people. He and the others had done it any number of times. If you think you are going to be eaten, you protect yourself somehow. It probably looked like a duty. I thought of Jesus's words when he was about to leave his disciples: "The time is coming when anyone who kills you will suppose that he is performing a religious duty. They will do these things because they do not know either the Father or me. I have told you all this so that when the time comes for it to happen you may remember my warning" (John 16:2–3 NEB).

"The time is coming. . . . Remember my warning." How safe are we? The five men had been missionaries, not cannibals. They had gone into Auca territory to take the gospel there, not to eat Indians. They loved God. They trusted him. They had prayed for protection, guidance, and success, and they had put their faith in him as shield and defender. As we, their wives, prayed with them over every step of the preparations for this venture, we thought surely God would protect and guide and give success. But it was the Indians who had the success. They won.

What then is faith? What in heaven's name do we mean when we say, "In God we trust"?

Dr. James I. Packer, in his book *God's Words*, says "the *popular* idea of faith is of a certain obstinate optimism: the hope, tenaciously held in face of trouble, that the universe is fundamentally friendly and things may get better."

I would have had to be an optimist of the most incorrigible obstinacy to have held on to that sort of faith in the dark times of my own life. It has been another faith that has sustained me—faith in the God of the Bible, a God, as someone once put it, not small enough to be understood but big enough to be worshipped.

I grew up with the Bible. I learned what faith is through the example of my parents and many other godly people. I went to Sunday school, church, missionary conferences, a Christian high school and college, and a Bible school. I yielded heart and life to Christ at an early age.

But when I arrived in Ecuador as a missionary, well prepared, I felt, for whatever lay ahead, my expectations were far from spiritually mature. Like Peter, I was still thinking as men think, not as God thinks. Peter recoiled in horror when his master explained what was to happen to Jesus when he got to Jerusalem. "Heaven forbid!" was Peter's response. "Nothing like that must happen to you!" Jesus turned to him with a devastating rebuke, identifying his disciple with Satan, because he stood in the way of obedience to the Father.

As I began mission work, I expected God to operate my way. "Heaven forbid that anything unfavorable should interrupt my work!" I expected him to do what I asked, not realizing what it means to pray, "Hallowed be thy name, thy kingdom come, thy will be done." I wanted God to explain himself to me when my expectations were turned upside down.

God knew what I really needed was not explanations but sanctification, *purifying*. My notions about myself, my work, and my God needed to be put through the fire. My heart needed deep and painful scouring. "Blessed are the pure in heart, for they shall see God."

As I studied the Bible and tried to obey it, I gradually saw that the God who is in charge has allowed all kinds of things to happen in the world that we would rather he had left out. Oh, we want our freedom, of course. Free will is a gift we would not wish to do without. Yet we wonder why God does not intervene in the exercise of *other* people's free will. Why are *they* allowed to cause war and misuse resources and make others suffer? Why are poverty, government corruption, tyranny, and injustice permitted to go on and on? Of course it is never our choices that are at stake here; it is other people's. We do not want God to curtail our freedom; we only want him to restrain others'.

My questions were not answered, but I wanted to "see" God, to know him. So I kept on reading the Book, kept trying to apply it to my life, kept bringing my own thinking and conduct under its authority, seeking God's meaning in every event that touched me, including Jim's death and other crises. As God had promised, his Word proved true. He instructed me. He kept me. He held me. He showed me all I *needed* to know for life and godliness, although he did not unfold all I *wanted* to know for understanding.

After Jesus had rebuked Peter for not thinking as God thinks, he went on to point out exactly what the cost of discipleship would be: the end of self, the acceptance of a cross, and unconditional obedience. "Whoever cares for his own safety is lost," he said (Matt. 16:25 NEB).

Does this mean there is no safety for us? Is there no sure protection for the godly? Note what Jesus said about Elijah: "[They] worked their will upon him; and in the same way the Son of Man is to suffer at their hands" (Matt. 17:12 NEB).

Evil men have often been permitted to do what they please. We must understand that divine permission is given for evil to work. To know the God of the Bible is to see that he who could have made automatons of all of us made instead free creatures with power and permission to defy him.

There is a limit, of course. Let us not forget this. The Tower of Babel was stopped. God has set limits on what man is allowed to do, but one day he put himself into men's hands. Jesus had sat in the temple teaching and nobody touched him, but the time came when the same people who had listened to him barged into Gethsemane with swords and cudgels. Jesus did not flee. He walked straight up to them. He was unconcerned about physical safety. His only safety was the will of the Father. "This is your moment," he said, "the hour when darkness reigns" (Luke 22:53 NEB).

Why did God make room for that moment? Why should there ever be an hour when darkness is free to rule?

When Jesus refused to answer Pilate the next morning, Pilate said, "Surely you know that I have authority to release you and I have authority to crucify you." Jesus's reply embraces the mystery of evil: "You would have no authority at all over me . . . if it had not been granted you from above" (John 19:10–11 NEB).

Every man and woman who chooses to trust and obey God will find his faith attacked and his life invaded by the power of evil. There is no more escape for us than there was for the Son of Man. The way Jesus walked is the way we must walk. Again and again we will find ourselves looking to heaven in bewilderment and asking the old question *why*.

In Jesus's last intimate discourse with his disciples before going to the cross, he seems to have drawn back a corner of the curtain for a moment to give them a glimpse of a profound truth that was still very far beyond them yet had tremendous implications for them, as well as for us. These were his words: "The Prince of this world approaches. He has no rights over me; but the world must be shown that I love the Father, and do exactly as he commands" (John 14:30–31 NEB). It is not an explanation of the mystery. It is a simple statement of fact and of duty: This is what will happen; therefore this is what I must do. Evil will come, but I must obey. The world must be shown.

The world's prince has power. That power does not nullify the will of the Father (it is still in effect), or defeat the obedience of the Son (he will go straight into the jaws of death). Nevertheless, the will of the Father, plus the obedience of the Son, plus the power of evil equaled the crucifixion. *The world must be shown.* Through that hideous punishment the world would be shown two things: the Son's love and his absolute obedience.

The lesson is thus set for Christ's followers: If we believe that God is God, our faith is not a deduction from the facts around us. It is not an instinct. It is not inferred from the happy way things work. Faith is a gift from God, and we must respond to him with a decision: The God of the universe has spoken, we believe what he says, and we will obey. We must make a decision that we will hold in the face of all opposition and apparent contradiction.

The powers of hell can never prevail against the soul that takes its stand on God and on his Word. This kind of faith overcomes the world. The world of today must be shown. We (you and I) must show them what Jesus showed the world on that dark day so long ago—that we love the Father and will do what he says.

What was it about the film *Chariots of Fire* that struck so many people? I believe it was the young man's clear commitment—uncompromising, unapologetic. We do not know much about that type of commitment nowadays. Here was a man determined to obey God, and nothing could shake that—not the Prince of Wales, the prospect of an Olympic medal, or world fame.

The one thing this young man cared passionately about was what Jesus cared about. That was what took five men into a place they well knew was dangerous. In each case a decision had been made long before that covered all subsequent decisions. These men trusted and were not afraid. They had found the only place of safety in all of earth or heaven, the Lord God himself.

"In the Lord I have found my refuge; why do you say to me, 'Flee to the mountains like a bird; see how the wicked string their bows and fit the arrow to the string, to shoot down honest men out of the darkness'?" (Ps. 11:1–2 NEB).

"Whoever cares for his own safety is lost; but if a man will let himself be lost for my sake, he will find his true self" (Matt. 16:25 NEB).

Letting go of what the world calls safety and surrendering to the Lord is our insurance of fulfillment. Christ knew his Father and offered himself unreservedly into his hands. If we let ourselves be lost for his sake, trusting the same God as Lord of all, we shall find safety where Christ found his, in the bosom of the Father.

Tenderness

There isn't a man or woman anywhere, I am convinced, who does not long for tenderness.

When I was in college, a girl who lived on my floor in the dormitory was pursued by a number of ardent young men on the campus. When the floor phone rang, we assumed it was for her. She was the kind who "could have anybody," it seemed, and treated most of them with casual carelessness. But one young man in particular would not be discouraged in his efforts to win her, even though she kept him at arm's length and declined some of his invitations. She made light of his attentions, as she did of many others', but was given pause one day when a bouquet arrived.

Like any woman, she eagerly snatched the card from its tiny envelope. Although one is supposed to be able to "say it with flowers," we all want plain English too.

On the card were two words: *Tenderly, Bill.*

I think it did her in. She was a buoyant, outgoing, attractive, sometimes flippant girl, but that word pierced the armor. When she showed it to me, it gave me a whole new vision, through a single powerful word, of what that man was made of. He was not handsome by any means. He was rather ordinary, in fact. But suddenly I saw him as strong and unusually desirable. I had not known that tenderness was an absolutely essential ingredient in a man, but I knew it at once, when I saw the card, and mentally added it to the list of qualifications I would need if I ever found a husband.

27

Parable in a Car Wash

My eighteen-month-old grandson Walter, his father, and I were out for a drive when his father decided it was time to have the car washed. Those automatic car washes can be a bit scary on the first run-through, even for an adult.

I watched Walter's face as the car was drawn into the dark tunnel. The water suddenly began to roar down over all four sides of the car, and his big blue eyes got bigger—but went immediately from the windows to the face of his father.

He was too small to understand what it was all about, and he'd had no explanation beforehand. What he did know was that Daddy would take care of him. Then the giant brushes began to close in around us, whirling and sloshing and making a tremendous racket. It grew even darker inside the car.

The boy had no way of knowing whether we'd get out of this alive. His eyes darted again from the brushes to the face of his father. I could see he was afraid, but he didn't cry.

Then the rubber wheel came banging down on the windshield, and hot air began to blast us. It must have seemed to the child that this tunnel had no end. What further terrors awaited us? He clung to only one thing; he knew his father. His father had never given him any reason not to trust him, but still. . . .

When the car finally broke out into sunshine, the little boy's face broke into a big smile. Everything was okay; Daddy knew what he was doing after all.

Like Walter, I have been through some dark tunnels. Although they were frightening, in the end I've found my heavenly Father always knows the way out.

Thirty years ago I was standing beside a shortwave radio in a house on the Atun Yacu, one of the principal headwaters of the Amazon, when I learned that my husband, Jim Elliot, was one of the five missionaries missing. They had gone into the territory of the Auca Indians, a people who had never heard even the name of Jesus Christ. What did I do? I suppose I said out loud, "O Lord!"

And he answered me. Not with an audible voice (I've never heard him speak that way in my life). But God brought to mind an ancient promise from the Book of Isaiah: "I have called you by name, you are mine. When you pass through the waters I will be with you; and through the rivers, they will not overwhelm you; when you walk through the fire you shall not be burned. . . . For I am the LORD your God" (Isa. 43:1–3 RSV).

I am the Lord your God. Think of it! The one who engineered this incredible universe with such exquisite precision that astronomers can predict exactly where and when Halley's comet will appear—this God is my Lord.

Evelyn Underhill said, "If God were small enough to be understood, He would not be big enough to be worshipped."

Can we imagine that God, who is concerned with so many stupendous things, can possibly be concerned about us? We do imagine it. We hope he is. That is why we turn to him in

147

desperation and cry out, as I did, "O Lord!" Where else can we possibly turn when we have come to the end of our resources?

Does God love us? Karl Barth, the great theologian, was once asked if he could condense all the theology he had ever written into one simple sentence.

"Yes," he said. "I can. 'Jesus loves me, this I know, for the Bible tells me so.'"

Think about the account of the crucifixion in Mark 15. Jesus was fastened to a cross. It was a man-made cross, and man-made nails were hammered through his hands—the hands that had formed the galaxies. Wicked men put him up there. Then they flung at him a bold and insolent challenge: "If you're the Son of God, come down! Then we'll believe."

Did he come down? No. He stayed there. He could have summoned an army of angels to rescue him, but he stayed there. Why? Because he loved us with a love that gives everything.

Because of the love of the Father for us, he gave his Son. Because of the love of the Son for his Father, he was willing to die, "so that, by God's gracious will, in tasting death he should stand for us all" (Heb. 2:9 NEB).

When I heard Jim was missing, my first response was "O Lord!" God answered by giving me a promise: "When you pass through the waters, I will be with you."

Was that enough for me? Was that all I wanted? No, I wanted Jim back alive. I didn't want to go through that deep river, that dark tunnel. Five days later I got another radio message: Jim was dead. All five of the men were dead.

God hadn't worked any magic. He is not a talisman, a magic charm to carry in our pocket and stroke to get whatever we want. He could have sent a rescue squad of angels to save Jim and the others, but he didn't. Why not? Didn't he love us?

Fourteen years later God brought another man into my life. I thought it was a miracle I'd gotten married the first time! Now, once again, I was a wife.

However, Addison Leitch and I had not yet reached our fourth anniversary when we learned he had cancer. *O Lord*, I thought, *another dark tunnel.* The medical verdict was grim, but we prayed for healing. We did not know positively what the outcome would be, but like little Walter, we knew our Father. We had to keep turning our eyes from the frightening things to him, knowing him to be utterly faithful.

Whatever dark tunnel we may be called upon to travel through, God has been there. Whatever deep waters seem about to drown us, he has traversed. Faith is not merely "feeling good about God" but a conscious choice, even in the utter absence of feelings or external encouragements, to obey his Word when he says, "Trust me." This choice has nothing to do with mood but is a deliberate act of laying hold of the character of God whom circumstances never change.

Does he love us? *No, no, no* is what our circumstances seem to say. We cannot deduce the fact of his unchanging love from the evidence we see around us. Things are a mess. Yet to turn our eyes back to the cross of Calvary is to see the irrefutable proof that has stood all the tests of the ages: "It is by this that we know what love is: that Christ laid down his life for us" (John 3:16 NEB).

We are all little Walters to God. He knows the necessity of the "car wash," the dark passages of every human life, but *he* is in the car! The outcome will be most glorious.

28

Two Marriageable People

What Holly thought would be an ordinary Sunday evening turned into an enchanted evening. She met Scott.

"I'd seen him around church a few times, but it's a big church and we had never spoken. During the social hour following the service we got into conversation. He offered to drive me home, and—well, you know the story. He started calling me, we'd talk for hours on the phone. He decided to join the singles group, hung around afterward and we'd talk, and finally he actually asked me out. Sometimes he picked up the tab, but usually I paid my own way. I didn't want to feel obligated to him.

"Once when we had dinner together he prayed," Holly confided to me, "thanking God for our friendship and for the fact that the singles group could witness a man and a woman who could be good friends without falling in love."

Without falling in love. Uh-huh. I've heard that story from both men and women, perhaps hundreds of times.

Who did Scott think he was kidding? Had it not crossed his mind that *one* of them might fall? One of the two always does. Poor Holly had fallen flat. She was in her early twenties and attractive, yet she told me she "had a problem." She did—her heart was on hold.

When one's heart is on hold, you do what Holly did—a lot of praying and crying and hoping for the telephone to ring. Scott kept her hopes up. He invited her to a big family wedding, even to the reception meant only for family and close friends. Surely he must be getting on toward serious. Would he put words to his feelings? Well, almost. He talked about marriage, telling Holly he often dreamed of having a wife and how he hoped to find one. He told her how much he wanted children, offering her his ideas on raising them. The time came when Holly could stand it no longer.

They were eating pizza by the fire in her living room. Scott always accepted her invitations. Once or twice he had brought flowers or a bottle of wine.

Tonight he was enjoying the pizza, chattering away about a game he'd been to. But Holly's mind wasn't on the game.

"Scott," she said hesitantly, "we need to talk about something."

"Yeah?"

"I mean—like, we've been, you know, *friends* long enough."

The man was startled. He took a huge bite of pizza and said nothing.

"This is really hard for me to say, but, Scott, if you don't have any intentions of, well, a real relationship, I can't spend any more time alone with you. I've felt so comfortable with you. I can be myself, you know? My real self, I mean. I've told you a lot of—well, of my *heart*. But if it doesn't—if you aren't, you know. . . ." Her voice trailed off.

The silence was thundering. Holly looked at Scott. Scott looked at the fire. After another bite and another gulp he said he couldn't see himself married to her. The truth was, of course, that for months Holly had been seeing herself married to him. To her, a "real relationship" meant engagement, although she didn't use that word. In fact, she told me, she had never voiced any desire whatsoever to be married to him. Hadn't she? Scott might be a little obtuse, but he knew what a "real relationship" had to mean. He thought he was forestalling any such complication by telling Holly about his hopes. Didn't she catch on that *she* wasn't what he was looking for?

So here are two marriageable people who would like to be married, though not in both cases to each other. What's wrong? Both the why and the how, it seems to me, are wrong.

Note that Scott took no risks, as far as he knew. Talked to a girl after church, drove her home—pretty innocuous, spur-of-the-moment gestures. Nobody would make anything out of that. She was nice and let him talk about what interested him. So he started going to the singles group, talked to a few others, phoned Holly now and then, went to dinner and let her pay her half (didn't want her to "think anything," didn't want to put her down by turning down her offer to pay). Then, because once or twice he thought maybe he caught a little glimmer in her eyes, he put across an important message—in a *prayer*. She couldn't suspect any nefarious designs here, could she? When he took her to the family wedding, she should have known she was just a sister to him.

She didn't. It was quite out of the question for her *not* to think of marriage. Any smallest sign of a man's interest was a big thing. She tried to deny it, tried to tell herself not to "think anything," but she couldn't refrain.

The man didn't mean to put her heart on hold. How did it happen? Had he wronged her? Was he being dishonest, unfair? What was he supposed to do—take 'em *all* out, give 'em equal time? He was no Casanova, just an ordinary guy. He meant well. He'd tried to play it cool. *The trouble is you can't play it cool with a powder keg.*

I wonder if it isn't time for Christian young people to discard the currently accepted methods of mate-finding, which haven't scored higher in marital success than the ancient matchmaker method. I offer the following as humble suggestions for the *why* and the *how* of finding a mate. They don't constitute the Law of Sinai, but I ask you to think soberly, even to pray, about them.

You men are the ones on whom God originally laid the burden of responsibility as head, initiator, provider. *Why* do you want to marry? If Scott had given sufficient thought and prayer to that one, perhaps he would not have been the bull in the china shop of Holly's heart. God ordained marriage. God provided the equipment needed for reproduction. But it is not his plan for every man to marry. How about getting down to business, when you reach the age of responsibility, and specifically asking God whether marriage is, in fact, a part of his plan for you? In order to listen to him without distraction you will need to:

1. Stop everything—intimacy, dating, any "special relationship."
2. Be silent before God. Lay your life before him, willing to accept the path he shows you. If you get no answer, do nothing in that direction now. *Wait.*
3. If it seems the answer is yes, go to a spiritual mother or father (someone older in the faith than you are, someone with wisdom and common sense who knows how to pray) and ask them to pray with you and for you about a wife. Listen to their counsel. If they know somebody they think suitable, take them seriously.
4. Study the story of Abraham's servant who was sent to find a wife for Isaac (Gen. 24). He went to the logical place where he might find women. He prayed silently, watched quietly. The story is rich in lessons. Find them.
5. Keep your eyes open—in your own "garden." You don't have to survey all the roses before you pick *the* one for your bud vase. When you spot the sort of woman you think you're looking for, watch her from a respectful

distance. Much can be learned without conversation, let alone "relationship." Ask about her of others who know her and whom you can trust to keep their mouths shut. Does she give evidence of being a godly woman? A womanly one? Expect God to lead. "Let the one to whom *I* shall say . . . let her be the one whom *thou* hast appointed" (Gen. 24:14 RSV).

6. Proceed with extreme caution, praying over every move. By this I do not mean mumbling prayers while you're charging across the church campus to ask her for a date. I mean giving yourself whatever it takes, whether weeks or years, to take his yoke and learn of him. It is "*good* for a man that he bear the yoke in his youth."

7. Talk to her in a casual setting. You will be able to discover if she is a woman of serious purpose. Do not mention "relationships," marriage, feelings.

8. Give yourself time to think. Go back to your spiritual mother or father. (In our family, our own parents were our spiritual parents as well, and they prayed for four specific people to marry four of their children. It happened.)

I'm not going to outline the chronology of dating. I would only suggest that you start small—a simple lunch somewhere rather than a gala dinner. *You* pick up the tab. Treat her like a lady, act like a gentleman. (See my book *The Mark of a Man* for more guidelines.)

If you find yourself falling for a girl who offers you only casual friendship, or worse, the cold shoulder, first get it settled with God that she is the one to pursue. Even if a woman tells a man to "get lost" but he knows in his heart she's the right one, he can still wait and pray for God's timing. I know of many married couples whose courtship began this way.

The time will come when your conversations have revealed, without direct inquiry, whether this woman would be prepared to accept your destiny and your headship; whether she is maternal, a homeworker—in short, whether she is what you've been praying for.

It is a great mistake to put too much stock in physical beauty or in thrills and chills. Neither has anything to do with a sound foundation for a marriage. Remember that the love of 1 Corinthians 13 is action, not a glandular condition. The love that makes a marriage is basically a deep respect and an unselfish kindness. That's pleasant to live with.

Now a few words, and only a few, for you women. I know—oh, how well I know—your position. Because we are women, we are made to be responders, not initiators (see *Let Me Be a Woman*). This means that the burden of responsibility of seeking and wooing a mate does not belong to us. To us belongs the waiting.

This does not mean inactivity. It means first of all a positive, active placing of our trust in him who loves us, does all things well, and promises to crown us with everlasting joy. It means next a continued obedience in whatever God has given us to do today, without allowing our longing to "slay the appetite of our living," as Jim Elliot once wrote to me, long before God gave us the green light to marry. It means just what Paul meant when he wrote from prison to the Philippian Christians, "Don't worry over anything whatever; tell God every detail of your needs in earnest and thankful prayer, and the peace of God, which transcends human understanding, will keep constant guard over your hearts and minds as they rest in Christ Jesus."

Often the awkward scenario depicted in Holly and Scott's story is more the woman's fault than the man's. That is because women generally allow too many liberties, make themselves too available, and press for explanations when they should remain quiet. It is foolhardy to stick your neck out that way. When *your* heart is on hold, it's best quietly to decline any further invitations rather than to try to "preserve the friendship." It can't be done. Better to simply back off.

If our supreme goal is to follow Christ, the rule of our lives will be *my life for yours*. We will be directing our energies far more toward the will of God and the service of others than to our own heart's longings. And that, believe me, is the best possible training course for marriage.

29

Pick Up the Broom!

Four more days until she would be seventeen. It would be her father's birthday too, but there would be no celebration this year. It was the depth of the Great Depression and her father was dying. The children knelt around his bed while their mother prayed, but the girl wondered whether anyone was listening. Was God near enough to hear a prayer? Did he take any notice of their situation?

On the day of the funeral it rained. Only the mother's friends came—the father's didn't bother. The girl, who was working as a maid, had to borrow a dress for the occasion. When they returned to the empty house, the sense of desolation was nearly overwhelming. But the widow, who had been silent for three days, went into the kitchen, picked up her broom, and began to sweep.

"I cannot explain how that action and that soft *whisk-whisk* sound gave me courage to go on," the girl wrote many years later. "My mother was now the head of the house, and we followed. We did not sit down and ask, 'What next? What will we do?' Our home was mortgaged and my father's lawyer stole her property. She walked out of his office a penniless widow with seven children, ages eight to eighteen. Later someone asked my mother how she had stood it. The answer was simple: 'I prayed.'"

The combination of prayer and faithful carrying out of duty has been balm to many when all hope has seemed to dissolve. The Word of the Lord came to Ezekiel: "I am taking from you at one blow the dearest thing you have, but you must not wail or weep or give way to tears. Keep in heart; be quiet, and make no mourning for the dead" (Ezek. 24:15–17 NEB). God denied Ezekiel the usual expressions of mourning and told him he was not to "eat the bread of despair." Ezekiel's response was, in effect, *Yes, Lord.* "I spoke to the people in the morning," Ezekiel said, "and that very evening my wife died. Next morning I did as I was told." Obedience was his consolation.

So the psalmist also found it: "Happy are they who obey his instruction.... In thy statutes I find continual delight.... I will run the course set out in thy commandments, for they gladden my heart" (Ps. 119:2, 16, 32 NEB). Happiness, delight, gladness—where can they come from when the world has fallen in?

A study of this psalm reveals the psalmist's firsthand knowledge of nearly every sort of human woe. For each he finds the same comfort: the Word of the Lord, variously called "commandments," "instruction," "counsel," "law," "statutes," "truth."

He understood the sense of alienation all of us experience: "I am but a stranger here on earth." He knew unfulfilled desire: "My heart pines with longing." He had been "put down": "set me free from scorn and insult ... the powers that be sit scheming together against me." He knew all about the sense of utter desolation: "I lie prone in the dust ... I cannot rest for misery." He had been persecuted: "Bands of evil men close round me.... Proud men blacken my name with lies."

The one who wrote this psalm had plenty of reason, humanly speaking, to feel very sorry for himself. But it is not self-pity that prompts him to list his troubles. It is rather a candid assessment, in the presence of the Lord, of the truth of his situation, each item on his list followed by prayer for the particular help needed or by a renewed affirmation of trust in the Word of his God.

The one who is called "a roaring lion" (1 Peter 5:8) knows well that his prey will be much easier to catch when weakened by sorrow or trouble of any kind. The woman with the broom shamed that lion. She did not "faint in the day of adversity," collapse in a heap, or wallow in a slough of self-pity. She knew where to find the strength to carry on. She went there at once and received the power which, as the apostle Paul discovered, "comes to its full strength in weakness."

In the same way I have been rescued from the lion's claws when everything in me said, *"You can't take this."* I woke one morning in a tiny temporary leaf shelter in Ecuador's jungle to find rain falling in solid sheets. The river had risen dangerously. The thought of trying to pack up in the downpour, get into a dugout canoe with my little daughter, and be poled up another river all day long to a remote clearing was too bleak. I was lonely, desolate, trapped. But that "Amazing Grace" that had brought me safe thus far reminded me of what I should do. I looked up to the Lord. "Lo, I am with you all the days" came the word. *All* the days, no matter what the weather, or how total the isolation. I took heart and, like the woman with the broom, did the next thing, which was to pack up and get myself and Valerie into the canoe. I think it rained all day, but it didn't matter, for the weather in my soul had cleared up.

A wonderful thing happens when we turn to the Lord and "pick up the broom." We find, as the palmist found, that "this day, as ever, thy decrees stand fast; for all things serve thee" (Ps. 119:91 NEB).

30

A Jungle Grave

Kimu's bare feet were planted firmly on the floor of the dugout canoe in front of me, as if the balls of the feet were bolted. His heels rose and fell as he raised his arms and plunged the pole to the bottom of the shallow river, rhythmically, steadily. Many times I had been fascinated by the strength and stability of Indian feet, standing in canoes, moving over trails, hanging from hammocks in the firelight. They were thick, square-toed, making the pale narrow feet of the white man, with the toes bent and crushed by years of confinement in shoes, seem pathetically deformed by comparison.

The canoe tipped and jerked at times with the motion of the poling or the river's current rushing against a fallen log. But Kimu's balance was perfect. The pole plunged, swung out, dripped softly, plunged. Kimu's shoulder muscles shifted effortlessly and his powerful thighs became taut as he pulled the canoe forward.

We were traveling the Anangu River in eastern Ecuador. I was watching, without very much hope, for signs of wildlife in the reeds along the shores. The light knocking and scraping of canoe poles, the voices of the men as they shouted taunts at the parrots that flew over or made ribald jokes to one another, warned most creatures of our approach. Besides this, my eyes were not trained as an Indian's eyes are to see things in the jungle. On a previous occasion the Indians had tried to point out to me an alligator which, they said, lay directly beneath my gaze on the river bottom. The water was not more than five feet deep and seemed perfectly clear. The Indians stopped the canoe, pointed with their poles. "There, senora! Right there." I saw nothing. Then with an astonishingly slow and deliberate jab, one of the men impaled the alligator on the end of his fish spear and brought it to the surface.

Another time my guides yelled, "There goes a boa!" I looked quickly where they pointed but did not see so much as the movement of a leaf where it had disappeared. It was as big as a man's thigh, they said.

Now this morning we saw only birds and the tracks of tapir and peccary. The forest moved slowly by on either side of the narrow river. The water was shallow in most places, with a bright sandy floor, and the Indians saw fish now and then, but even these escaped me. At the bends of the river the water deepened into lucid green pools beneath rock walls which were hung with mosses and orchids. Here we heard the sudden strong purr of hummingbirds' wings.

The morning was still and sunny. Except for the mild discomfort of my seating arrangement—two sticks wedged across the canoe—I felt almost a sense of beatitude. There was not a single human habitation on the entire length of this jungle river, and its primeval peace entered into me. The awareness that we were the only human beings anywhere around made me reluctant to violate the silence, even when I saw a bird or animal track I wanted to ask about.

We soon reached the mouth of the Anangu and moved on into the Curaray, a wider, more sluggish stream. I thought of the first time I had seen this river. It was over five years ago, from thousands of feet up in the air. Four other widows and I were being flown by the U.S. Air Rescue Service over the scene where Kimu and five fellow tribesmen had killed our husbands a few days before. We had knelt on the floor of the C-47, straining our eyes through the tiny windows toward the billowing forest below. There was nothing to see, really. The immense vista of jungle was unrelieved except for this winding river with its white stretches of beach. When the plane began to circle, we knew which beach it had been. It was just like the others, except that we could discern the remains of a little airplane on the sand. We flew back to the air base, and I remember asking myself what I suppose thousands who are newly bereaved must ask: How is it that the sun shines today? It is as bright and cheerful as it was last week, when they were all alive.

Now, traveling down this same river by canoe, it looked as it had looked from the air, like countless other rivers in the Amazon rain forest. I had been up and down it a dozen times in the past three years but had never been as far as the beach we had seen from the plane. We were going now to visit that beach.

We had left home—a small jungle clearing with eight thatched houses—just after dawn and hiked over the trail to where the canoes lay tied. An hour's walk from home I suddenly thought of matches. I had become so accustomed to depend on the Indians for all that we would need on the trail that I seldom packed more than blanket and clothes for myself and my daughter Valerie. The Indians hunted and fished, cooked the food, and we all ate together; they built shelters for us all to sleep in. But inevitably the Indians were beginning to count on some civilized conveniences, and suppose this time they had expected me to bring the matches? I asked if they had any. No—hadn't I brought any? When I admitted that I hadn't, they laughed. Kimu slung down his carrying net beside the trail. "Let me go get some," he said. This seemed a big thing to ask, but it was nothing to him. Back over the trail he went for what had been an hour's walk for us, another hour to retrace his steps. We went on, expecting to wait for him at the river, but just as we reached it, exactly one hour after he had left us, he stepped out of the trees behind us, smiling his benign smile. He said nothing. I couldn't say anything either, for his language has no words for thank you or sorry.

In the canoe was Benito, a member of the Quichua tribe, who live nearest to the Aucas. He would have killed Kimu on sight a few years before. Now he stood on the flat tail of the canoe, poling, shouting to Kimu in Kimu's language. Benito's wife, Gimari, an Auca woman, sat behind the food and blankets that were piled on a bamboo platform in the center of the craft. She had been one of three Auca Indians who made a friendly visit to the camp where my husband Jim and his four friends were, two days before they died. She had said she would show me just where she had first glimpsed the foreigners through the trees.

I was not sure there would be any beach left. Jungle rivers change with every heavy rain. The sand shifts, logs are carried downstream and lodged in new positions each time, piling up debris and making new islands. The channels swerve from one side to the other, banks cave in. Yet nothing really changes. No bridges span them, no dams choke them—except the little split-bamboo and rock dams that Indians build in order to position the water for a day's fishing. We passed several campsites where Quichuas had left flimsy reed shelters on these expeditions. They would be washed away in the next swelling. We had slept in such shelters many times and had nearly been washed away ourselves once when the river flooded at midnight. Valerie, now six years old, looked longingly at these cute little houses as we passed and wondered why we couldn't stop and spend the night in one of them. I explained that we would be stopping when it was time to sleep. But we wanted to get farther downriver this afternoon.

About midmorning the polers were thirsty. They beached the canoe, and Gimari broke open a leaf packet of *chicha*, as it is called in Spanish. In this case it was a mass of cooked manioc root, masticated and slightly fermented, which Gimari squeezed by the fistful into a gourd of water and offered to each of the men first, and then to us. Val drank in great greedy gulps, the lumps and strings in the milky fluid bothering her not at all. I had learned to appreciate the refreshment if not the consistency of this highly nourishing food and was only too glad to be spared the endless fuss of the American-style picnic. There is no packing and unpacking of utensils, no dishwashing, no time wasted. It does not take long to see the common sense of the Indian way.

When everyone had taken on sufficient fuel, we climbed back into the canoe and sailed on.

Distances on the rivers are measured by curves. Indians' landmarks are species of trees, deep places in the water, or places where so-and-so was speared or where they just missed the herd of wild hogs on the trip before last. I gave up long ago trying to follow their descriptions of locations. One curve is like the next one to me; even the trees have little to distinguish them, being so nearly obliterated by masses of lianas and air plants. Every twenty minutes or so we rounded a new curve—a strip of sand on the right, a wall of forest on the left; then a strip of sand on the left, a wall on the right. Curve after curve, the river doubling back on itself so as nearly to cut through the narrow neck of land that formed the curve in some places.

At about two o'clock we saw ahead of us a long straight stretch of water, with a long straight stretch of sand at the right. The Indians gently slid the canoe onto the upper point of this beach, threw down their poles, and jumped out. No one said anything, but I deduced that this must be the place.

"This?" I asked.

"This," they said. They started walking down the beach. I followed. This was where Jim had died. He was buried somewhere here. Hundreds of times I had tried to reconstruct in my imagination the scene that took place here. I had seen the colored slides and movie film the men had made here. I had read their diaries of events that led up to their deaths. The six Auca Indians who had killed them were now my friends, and they had told me quite candidly all that happened.

My thoughts were immediately distracted by a jaguar. I could hardly believe it. He shot from a pile of immense logs that lay along the sand and bounded with long, slow leaps toward the forest, looking over his shoulder at us. It was the first one I had ever seen in the jungle. I was stupefied. None of the others saw it, and I could think of neither the Quichua nor the Auca word for jaguar and could only shout, "What is it?" Finally the Indians saw it too and raced after it. No one had a gun, or even a blowgun, and it was too far away from Kimu to throw his spear. Of course it disappeared long before we reached the place where it had lain, probably asleep, under the huge logs. We examined the footprints. I remembered then a phrase from a little note Jim had written to me from the tree house at this beach, flown out to me a few days before he died. "Saw lots of puma tracks this morning—some as big as a woman's hand." There they were. (The Quichua word *puma* means any kind of jungle cat.)

The Indians laughed, chided one another for being unarmed, and speculated as to where it had gone and what it had said when it saw us. They followed the spoor to the edge of the forest, where it vanished.

I wondered, absurdly, if it might be the same puma whose tracks Jim had seen. At first the animal had seemed a thing incredible, almost a specter. What business had it there? Now it appeared a link with the past.

Benito had wandered farther down the beach, and I saw that he was digging in the sand.

"Airplane," he said. There was a piece of aluminum sticking up a few inches out of the sand, with a rusted red scrap of metal bolted to it. I knelt down and examined it. It was from Nate Saint's airplane, a piece that fitted above the door. The ceaseless rise and fall of the river had buried the rest of the plane. Nate had flown each of the other four men in here, one by one, with all of their gear, which included the boards for a tree house. It took highly skilled flying to get down into this canyon of trees and land on a two-hundred-yard sandspit.

Kimu waved toward the trees downriver. "That's where the plane came—*bbbbb*—right over those trees. Then it went out there" (gesturing in the opposite direction), "*bbbb*—and flew away to where we couldn't see it, where it looks blue, far away."

When the Aucas killed the five, they stripped the fabric from the plane, "because we thought it might fly home by itself," they explained to me.

I asked Gimari where she had first stepped out of the jungle to greet the foreigners. She pointed across the river.

"Your husband saw us. He came across and led us over here." She laughed.

"And the men, when they came to spear, where did they come from?"

"The same place," she said. "They watched the men in secret for two days. Then they brought women with them. The women wanted to see the foreigners too. They came out first and sat down—here, here on the beach. The men had built a little house here to cook in, so the women fanned the foreigners' fire. The foreigners sat down too, and they all laughed together. They ate some meat and some wasp's nest [this is the Auca word for bread]. Akawu, my mother, fanned the fire—*wih, wih, wih, wih*, she fanned. Then suddenly, Gikita and Minkayi jumped out with spears. Dyuwi and Nimunga and Kimu leaped out—from right over there. They speared all of them."

She was very casual and pleasant about it all.

One of the Indians asked if I wanted to see where the men were buried. Yes, I wanted to see, though I knew there was nothing there. Valerie saw us walking back up the beach and raced over breathlessly. This trip was a lark for her. I had told her of course that we were going to where her friends had killed her father. But since she had no recollection of him, this meant little, while any trip by trail or canoe with the Indians meant much. But now she wanted to know when we were going to see her daddy. I explained that we were not going to see him—not, that is, until we saw him in God's house—but we would see the place where other missionaries had buried him.

The Indians led me to the reeds at the edge of the forest and broke through them a few feet to a spot a little higher than the level of the river.

"Here." One of them pointed. I saw a slight depression in the ground, covered by a heavy growth of reeds. Buried here were four men: Roger Youderian from Montana, Pete Fleming from Seattle, Nate Saint from Philadelphia, and Jim, my husband, who was from Portland, Oregon. The body of Ed McCully from Milwaukee had not been found. The Curaray had washed it away before the search party reached the scene.

Wordsworth's simple words about Lucy came to me:

> But she is in her grave, and oh,
> The difference to me!

My reflections were brief. Kimu picked up a scrap of aluminum nailed to a rotted two-by-four, remains of the tree house the foreigners had built.

"Ah! Here's a fine piece of tin for me to mend my canoe with!" he said. To him, this was worth coming for. The others kicked around in the bush hunting for more. There was nothing, except a very rotten stump nearby, which they said was once the tree where the house had been. The jungle had reduced everything to indistinguishability.

We went back into the sunlight of the riverside. The water flowed deeper and more smoothly here than farther up. It was placid and silent, and I found it difficult to imagine the power that was generated during floods, great enough to have brought down that giant tree, probably eight or ten feet in diameter, and deposited it where it lay lengthwise along the sand.

It was even more difficult to imagine that anything of any significance had ever happened at this quiet place. This thought was immediately followed by the realization that after all, of those present I was the only one to whom what had happened held any significance. Several of the Indians were poking around in the sand searching for turtle eggs. Val was chasing a puppy that had come with us.

I looked at Kimu, whose tally of people speared included his own parents-in-law. He stood quietly waiting for the rest of us, holding upright in front of him a palmwood lance that matched those used on the five Americans. He had taken out of his earlobes the white balsawood plugs which formerly, with a piece of string around his loins, had been the sum total of his costume. The great gaping holes left by the plugs did nothing to enhance his appearance, nor did the baggy blue trunks he was now wearing in imitation of the Quichuas. But the breadth and power of his chest and arms made it easy for me to imagine his throwing that spear, while at the same time the gentleness and serenity of his expression made it unthinkable that he could ever have used it on a human being.

Like Kimu, the jungle was imperturbable. The sand, which it seemed to me ought somehow to bear indestructible scars of the fantastic scene, was washed clean. I thought of the accounts which two of the killers had recorded on tape for me, giving their versions of what took place that Sunday afternoon five years before. They had sat in my hammock and taken the microphone as casually as the most seasoned commentator. They had described, play by play, what they did—who speared whom (designating the victims as "the tall one," or "the one with black hair," or "the hairy one") and how many blows it took them to die; how the foreigners had jumped into the river or run into the forest with spears lodged in their bodies; how they had returned to their companions on the beach and the Aucas had yanked out the spears and rammed them in again; how, when the Aucas saw that they were all dead or nearly so, they looked over their belongings, appropriating what they thought might be useful, throwing the useless things such as guns and cameras into the river; how they had returned to their families to tell them that there was no longer any danger of being eaten since they had made a clean sweep of the people who came in the airplane. It was all in a day's work.

To the Indians the incident was over. Not to me ("oh, the difference!"), and not to God. He is the Author of the whole human story. It is not yet finished. On another level the terrible facts acquire a wholly different light:

> Then I heard a voice in heaven proclaiming aloud: "This is the hour of victory for our God, the hour of his sovereignty and power, when his Christ comes to his rightful rule! For the accuser of our brothers is overthrown, who day and night accused them before our God. By the sacrifice of the Lamb they have conquered him, and by the testimony which they uttered; for they did not hold their lives too dear to lay them down. Rejoice then, you heavens and you that dwell in them! But woe to you, earth and sea, for the devil has come down to you in great fury, knowing that his time is short!"
>
> Revelation 12:10–12 NEB

Kimu looked questioningly at me and smiled patiently.

"Waeniya?" he said, using the name the Indians had given me. "Let's go."

"Let's go," I said.

There was no reason to stay. We drank some more *chicha*, got into the canoe, and headed back up the Curaray. The Indians wanted to reach a certain shelter for the night, so we must hurry. And perhaps there would be fish or a tapir to catch on the way.

Elisabeth Elliot is one of the most loved and respected Christian communicators of our day and is the author of more than twenty books, including *Through Gates of Splendor, Shadow of the Almighty, The Path of Loneliness, Passion and Purity, Let Me Be a Woman*, and *A Path through Suffering*.

After eleven years of missionary work in Ecuador, South America, she returned to the United States and continued writing and speaking. Elliot was adjunct professor at Gordon-Conwell Seminary for four years and writer-in-residence at Gordon College for another four years. She and her husband, Lars Gren, live in Magnolia, Massachusetts.